Tormented Minds

Christine Roberts

intellect™
Bristol, UK
Portland, OR, USA

First published in UK in 2003 by
Intellect Books, PO Box 862, Bristol BS99 1DE, UK

First published in USA in 2003 by
Intellect Books, ISBS, 920 NE 58th Ave. Suite 300, Portland, Oregon 97213-3786, USA

Anyone wishing to perform any of the plays published in this anthology should
contact Christine Roberts for permission, at the following address:
Christine Roberts (Hall),
Senior Lecturer in Theatre and Performance,
Faculty of Arts and Humanities,
University of Plymouth,
Douglas Avenue,
Exmouth,
EX8 2AT
Devon.

Series Editor: Roberta Mock
Copy Editor: Julie Strudwick

Front cover:
Original photograph by Sarah Swainson (Copyright © 1998).
Mise-en-scene: Roberta Mock.
Cover design: Paul Prudden.

A catalogue record for this book is available from the British Library

ISBN 1-84150-081-X

Printed in Great Britain by The Cromwell Press, Wiltshire.

Contents

Acknowledgements

Part One

Adrian Fortescue's *Ceremonies of the Roman Rite Described* was the standard Roman Catholic ceremonial manual for almost fifty years from 1917. Revised several times by Canon J. B. O'Conell after Fortescue's death in 1923, the last edition was published in 1962 and later republished by The Saint Austin Press. The author wishes to thank the publisher for permission to use sections of the text in *Ceremonial Kisses*.

Part Two

'*Shading the Crime*: Acting Hopelessness as an Act of Hope' by Christine Roberts and Roberta Mock was originally published in *Studies in Theatre Production*, number 19, June 1999.

Part Three

Details of Sor Juana's life and the original poetry extracts have been taken from the following sources.The author wishes to thank the publishers for their permission to use these details in the text of *The Maternal Cloister*:

Paz, O. (1988) *Sor Juana Or, The Traps of Faith*. Trans. M. Sayers Peden. Cambridge, Mass.: The Belknap Press of Harvard University Press.

Sor Juana Ines de la Cruz (1985) *Sor Juana Ines de la Cruz. Poems. A Bilingual Anthology*. Trans. M. Sayers Peden. Arizona State University,Tempe, Arizona, USA: Bilingual Press/Editorial Bilingue.

Christine Roberts translated elements of Sor Juana's original poetry into English.

'*The Maternal Cloister*: The Manipulation of Sor Juana?' was originally written as a paper delivered at the International Federation for Theatre Research annual conference, 'Trans-actions: Culture and Performance', University of New South Wales, Australia (July 2001).

Part One

Ceremonial Kisses
Author's Introduction

Ceremonial Kisses explores the effect indoctrination and guilt can have on the development of a personality. Within the play we experience the increasing torment of the main character/Master of Ceremonies through the actions and presence of the Chorus/Choir.

The Chorus represent: the institution of the church; the main character's suppressed desires and his gradual descent. It is without specific gender – the scenes and roles in which it appears dictate the sex of the individuals within it. The Acolyte is both part of the Chorus and, at times, separate from it. He becomes the focus of the main character's increasing obsession with his own sexuality. He encounters the Acolyte through cottaging – the practice of picking up men for casual sex in toilets.

As the main character becomes more confused, so the role of the Chorus and Acolyte becomes more ambiguous. Do they really exist? Or are they an elaborate fantasy created by the Master of Ceremonies to further punish himself? Are they physical representations of his mind?

The play takes place in four locations, each with its own particular set of rituals: the church and the confessional; the supermarket aisles with its 'muzak' soundtrack; the gents' toilets adjoining the supermarket aisles and the cubicle and, the Master of Ceremony's home where his increasing isolation is epitomised by his obsession with television advertisements and the practice of 'zapping'.

As the Master of Ceremony's attempts to liberate himself leave him racked with guilt, so he is forced back to the solace of the confessional and absolution. The cycle continues and the demons remain.

Ceremonial Kisses

Ceremonial Kisses was premiered by Lusty Juventus at the Exeter & Devon Arts Centre on 21 September 1996, followed by a run at the Hackney Empire Studio Theatre, London (December 1996) with the following cast: James Barlow(The Acolyte); Misri Dey (Choir Member/Wife); Shad Khan (Choir Member); Rube (Choir Master); Mike Stoneham (Master of Ceremonies) and Ruth Way (Choir Member).

It was performed at the Edinburgh Festival 1997 and the Redgrave Theatre, Bristol, with Alistair Ganley as the Master of Ceremonies.
Co-directed by Roberta Mock and Christine Roberts. Design and construction by Sam Shaw. Choreography and vocal work by Misri Dey and Ruth Way. Lighting by Emma Pearce and Debbie Tyreman.

The Lusty Juventus production of Ceremonial Kisses, *December 1996.*
Photograph by Geraint Lewis.

The Characters

The Master of Ceremonies (M.C.) (a married man in his forties)
The Acolyte (a man in his early twenties)
The Chorus/Choir (group of three or more men and women)
The M.C.'s Wife (played by member of the chorus)

5

Scene One

(There is one cubicle on stage. This looks solid, but the walls are in fact stretched muslin or latex. There is an ambiguity about the set: basins which can be either stoups or washbasins; the drinks fountain doubles as a font, an altar with vases of flowers and cloths which can be used ritualistically, or literally, as towels. There is a vertical grid up Stage Left (SL).
The lighting defines three locations: church, toilet and supermarket. The cubicle is lit for the church. The light intensifies on these as the noise builds.
A quiet chanting can be heard. This begins at an indiscernible level and grows. Throughout the play, lines attributed to the chorus may be sung, chanted or spoken in unison or distributed to individuals as is deemed appropriate. The chorus is made up of choir members.)

ACOLYTE AND CHORUS
Red is for the feast of the Precious Blood,
For Martyr,
For Holy Innocent's Day.
Make a prostration,
If the Blessed Sacrament is exposed during the rite of Exposition
On entering or leaving the church.
To make the Sign of the Cross,
Place the left hand extended under the breast,
Hold the right hand extended also.
At the words *Patris*,
Raise it and touch forehead.
At *Filii* touch the breast at a sufficient distance down,
But above the left hand.
Choir, not necessarily those who sing,
So it was originally and in theory should still be so.
Do not place them either side of the altar,
It is not artistically effective to do so.
Servers.
They should avoid too much precision,
Or affectation,
Or such a bearing as befits soldiers on parade rather than Churchmen.
All must be done gravely and regularly;
But if behaviour is too punctilious and uniform
The sacred functions look too theatrical.
The normal place for the Acolytes
Is in front of the credence.
The Master of Ceremony should know what he has to do,
And the function of everyone else.

(As the volume of the voices increases the characters inside the cubicle begin to move, pushing hands/faces etc. against the walls. All characters come /climb out of cubicle except M.C.. These characters construct a series of religious

6

tableaux as the M.C. continues to speak. The M.C. becomes increasingly more frantic.)

M.C.
Those who are about to celebrate the holy mysteries must have confessed their sins, must be reconciled to all men and have nothing against anyone. Till the time of sacrifice they must keep their hearts from bad thoughts, be pure, and fast, until the moment arrives.
Bless me Lord for I have sinned!
Mea Culpa!
Guilt is an abstract which my religion makes concrete,
Something palpable,
Something tangible.
Mea Culpa!

(The CHORUS breaks from the tableaux and begins to climb around and over the cubicle until they are inside with the M.C. all pushing the walls.)

CHORUS
Secrets.
Say the secrets reading from the Missal.
Says these silently.
Only the first and last secrets have the conclusion,
Per Dominum Nostrum.
At the end of the last secret say the words of the conclusion
Spiritus Sancti Deus,
Silently.
Confess your sins with true sorrow.

M.C.
Absolution after confession.

(CHORUS move out of cubicle and take up one final tableau. ACOLYTE stays in the cubicle with M.C.. Lighting change for toilet. CHORUS move behind the grid and watch. ACOLYTE comes out of cubicle and exits SL. He is followed by the M.C. who washes his hands and then exits SL. Chorus slowly disappears, exiting from behind the grid.)

M.C.
Absolution after confession.

Scene Two

(Lighting change for supermarket. Muzak drifts out (possibly as well as an electronic bleeping noise). The CHORUS and ACOLYTE enter Stage Right (SR) with supermarket trolleys. M.C. and one of the CHORUS are clearly a couple,

this is emphasized by their interaction. The remaining CHORUS members and the ACOLYTE are characters in a supermarket.
The M.C.'s WIFE is the only one not relishing the atmosphere and is eager to buy what she needs and leave. Movement piece should emphasise the link between the tranquility of a church and the ritualistic element of supermarket shopping, using aisles and images in an ambiguous way. The characters can enter frenetically but should become unblinking and malleable. This should be seen as another refuge from the pressures outside, but it should also be clear that they are being manipulated by the experience.
The fourth wall can be utilised as imaginary shelves.)

ALL CHARACTERS EXCEPT WIFE
Big and bland and abundant,
Homogenized.
Cleanliness, convenience, availability.
Fruit market-stall freshness,
Not soiled.
Fish,
For the brain,
Without smell.
Flesh, meat, neat, bright, unstained, glossy, vacuum-packed, shimmering and
Bloodless.

WIFE
List?

M.C.
Spurlchase.

CHORUS
Resistance is entirely pointless,
In an hermetic world.
Hopeless...helpless.

WIFE
Middle-class, middle-brow...

CHORUS
...loyal!
It looks good.

WIFE
It's easy to produce!

CHORUS
It's fresh!

WIFE
Aroma management.

CHORUS
Impulsive, innovative.

WIFE
Brainwashed, seduced.
Numb feelings of power, without
Responsibility.

CHORUS
Seduction.
Numb feelings of power without,
Responsibility.
Sanctuary.

WIFE
Supermarkets!

CHORUS
Servicescapes.

WIFE
Shelves!

CHORUS
Stock Keeping Units.
SKUs.

WIFE
Needs!

CHORUS
Need state.
Dieting? Economising? Indulging? Impressing?
Hello! That looks good.

M.C.
Pasta! We need pasta…

CHORUS
Fusilli, Farfalle?
Rigate, Radiatore, Rigatoni…
Pappardelle, Vermicelli, Torchietti, Campanelle…
Tagliatte pagliae fieno!

WIFE
Shells...quick cook...
Beans...

CHORUS
Mixed in mild chilli sauce,
Mixed in spicy pepper sauce,
Mixed in sweet and sour...sauce.

Flageolet,
Aduki,
Borlotti,
Butter,
Broad,
Kidney,
Black eye,
Stringless
Haricots Verts!

WIFE
Baked.
Coffee...

CHORUS
Italian roast, Italian blend,
French roast, Mocha blend.
Kenyan blend, Colombian roast.
Cafetière and Percolator,
Espresso...

WIFE
Instant.

CHORUS
Meat!

German pepper salami,
Luke's Hogs sausage,
Kanos sausage...
Proscuitto di spech?
Sancisson sec?
Mortadella?
Pancetta?
Bresaola?
Felino?
Milano?
Chippolat...o ?

WIFE
Frozen.

CHORUS
Spinach and Ricotta Cheese, Cannelloni!
Seafood Linguini...
Pasta Penne Nicoise...
Spaghetti Puttanesca.
Deep Dish Duck Dupiaza,
Creamy Chicken Korma,
Mouthwatering, Microwaved...

WIFE
Peas.

M.C.
Treats?

CHORUS
Treats, treats, treats...

Five cranberry topped pork and turkey snack pies...
Six mini Isle of Skye smoked salmon en croute...
Dinner party Dim Sum selection...
Cocktail chicken satay.

Seven mini banoffe pies...
Seafood medley...
Filo parcels...
Vol-au-vents.

Ciabatta, cholla, sfilatino,
Bagels, pitta, petits pain...
Crusty rolls.

Two large tarts au citron...
Twenty crostini!

WIFE
Toilet paper.

CHORUS
Deep heat kumquats...
Party prickly pears...
Paw paw...
Lychees...loose.
Mangos, mini, medi, large...

Lollo Biondo, Lollo Rosso…
Oyster, horse, button, British, organic, shitake!

Single, double, dwarf, fine…
Snap, smooth, deep and firm.

Firm and sticky…medjool dates.

WIFE
Ajax?

CHORUS
Potato skins.

*(As the scene continues the M.C. becomes increasingly distracted. He kisses his WIFE, gives her flowers from the altar and moves SL. He slowly moves into space. Lighting indicates toilet.
CHORUS and ACOLYTE continue shopping etc.)*

M.C.
Convenient, clean and available.

(The M.C. washes his fingers and methodically dries them on the towel. He then stands provocatively in the doorway of the cubicle. The ACOLYTE breaks away from the CHORUS and enters.)

ACOLYTE
Sanctuary.

(ACOLYTE crosses to the cubicle and enters. M.C. follows him in.)

M.C.
Seduction.

(Lighting is on the cubicle and dim in the supermarket. Musak plays quietly in the background. The CHORUS and WIFE remain in the supermarket. ACOLYTE leaves cubicle followed by the M.C.. M.C. returns to his WIFE.)

WIFE
That was slick, I didn't see you disappear.

M.C.
Never fear.

WIFE
No dear.
Now can we get on…

I want to get out of here.

M.C.
Now?
Go?

WIFE
I've got everything we need.

M.C.
For Jim?
For Jean?
For Jo?

WIFE
Come on, let's go.
How many more have we got to feed?

M.C.
I thought I might stay.
Buy some…tools.

WIFE
Anything to linger,
You're behaving like a fool!

M.C.
OK, don't make a fuss.
I can come alone,
It's only an eight-minute drive…
From home.

WIFE
Eight minutes?
From home?

M.C. *(exiting with WIFE.)*
Yes.
I timed it one day.
Eight minutes.
So!

WIFE
Absolutely bloody vital to know!

(WIFE leaves with trolley, M.C. follows her. Lights fade as they exit SR.)

Scene Three

*(CHORUS form tableaux or cross-like shape. Lighting indicates church.
M.C. enters SL. He stops at basin /stoup and crosses himself with the water. He
then genuflects at altar and enters the cubicle/confessional.)*

CHORUS
Take the holy water from the stoup,
Make the sign of the cross.
In ceremonial entrances everybody genuflects.
Continue the custom of the church,
There is no good reason to change it.
Observe the rules which forbid certain ceremonies.
Observe the points – they make for reverence and decorum.
Confess,
Confessional –
Days and hours are fixed when these can be heard,
Order amongst the chaos.
Proper place for confession –
Church.
In a confessional.
Penance is the only sacrament administered sitting.
The penitent should make the sign of the cross
Then seek the blessing…
Dominus Sit A Corde Tuo.
Penitent speak the Confiteor.
Pray before telling your sins.
Confess to almighty God and to the Father.

M.C.
Bless me Lord for I have sinned.
I am filled with loathing and self-disgust at my actions.
But I am compelled –
I have no resistance.
Every time I commit the sin,
I vow not to do so again…

CHORUS
One can be absolved of ones sins only if they are not premeditated.
If you are overcome,
Overpowered by some,
Desperate urge,
And commit the sin,
You can be forgiven.
Your sins can only be forgiven if they are totally unpremeditated,
Without intention
Or design.

M.C.
I feel as if I'm being sucked down,
Sucked in.
I feel so desperate.
I am betraying my wife, my children,
I put my profession at risk.
I feel as if I am drawn to meet with devils –
Head on,
To confront the demons.
I commit obscene acts,
Am compelled to debase myself and others.
I relish the pain I inflict on others.
I delight in the pain I inflict on myself.
I consume and am consumed by the demons.
The feeling is intoxicating.
The greater the sense of danger,
The greater the fear of being caught.
So the desire is heightened.
The ecstasy!
The intensity of the guilt only seems to confirm the immediacy of the act.
The guilt itself is almost as pleasurable –
It is so…intense.
I am really aware of existing.
It is so palpable.
The ecstasy…

CHORUS
Before the fall.

M.C.
Mea culpa, mea culpa, mea culpa (beats chest and weeps).
The ecstasy before the fall.

CHORUS
We must observe rules which forbid certain acts.
There are strict rules to observe.
Rituals to perform which help control our behaviour,
To keep our free will within certain strict parameters.
Use these to help yourself –
To exercise control within the church
And you will find God's strength.
What is allowed?
What is permitted?
Temptation is the cloak of the devil.
The devil comes in many guises.
He comes to tempt you.
You are tempted with the promise of ecstasy –

Ecstasy without God will lead to the fall.
It will lead to damnation and the fires of hell.

But...
To fall to temptation is not a sin,
It is not final.

M.C.
No, to fall to temptation is not a sin.
I am after all human.

CHORUS
But a fall with no remorse,
Or sense of guilt,
Or repentance,
Cannot, and will not, be forgiven.
There can be no absolution without guilt and remorse.
How great is your sense of guilt.

M.C.
As great as the pleasure I experience.
The greater the pleasure,
The greater the guilt.

CHORUS
Sickness, sin and evil are what we encounter in life.
These men you desire are devils in disguise.
If you succumb...
Confutatis Maledictus –
You will be consigned to the flames of woe,
To fire which never dies – burning you forever.

Be thankful that we have the sacristy of the confession,
Absolution through guilt, repentance and confession.

M.C.
God the father of mercies through the death and resurrection of his son, has
reconciled the world to himself and sent the Holy Spirit among us for the
forgiveness of his sins.

CHORUS
Is the Lord in your heart?
Do you confess your sins with true sorrow?

M.C.
I do with true sorrow.

CHORUS
I absolve you from your sins in the name of
The Father and of The Son and of The Holy Spirit.
Amen.

M.C.
Thank you Father.

CHORUS
May you find comfort and protection in
The Seal of the Confession,
And in your absolution.

(The lights dim on confessional/church.)

Scene Four

*(Armchair and television centre-stage. M.C. sits in chair 'zapping' with his
remote control around the stations; he ends up watching the adverts. These
depict a range of scenes showing soft porn, food, and the idealised family. He
becomes increasingly more agitated.
In the background the dimly lit CHORUS process in SL with candles. They go
through a range of rituals, but they are all slightly wrong and with sexual
overtones. They stop at basins/stoups and one dips their finger into the water
which the other licks, they then make 'the sign of the cross'. They walk to the
altar and genuflect. They stand in front of the altar, in a group, back to
audience.
ACOLYTE enters SL and repeats the action. He walks to altar and prostrates
himself. M.C. never directly looks at the scene behind him; he is imagining it.)*

M.C.
Wrong, wrong, wrong.
You're doing it wrong!

*(M.C. begins zapping more frantically as he becomes more agitated.
The CHORUS turns around and gives the ACOLYTE communion. Again this is
done inaccurately and overtly sexually, and in parallel to the M.C.'s speech and
actions.)*

M.C.
It's all wrong!
It's got to be correct. Precise.
There are rules to be followed.

*(M.C. stands and faces the audience replicating their Communion moves –
accurately – but quite frenzied.)*

17

M.C.
At the Holy name, bow the head.
Bow the head!
Lean over the altar, to receive blessed Communion.
Do not extend the tongue.
Break the Sacred Species against the roof of the mouth,
Do not touch Him with the teeth.
Lay the Paten on the Corporal,
Rub fingers lightly over it.
Now stand upright...resting.
Meditate the most Holy Sacrament.
Holding hands raised and joined before the face.
Shut the eyes.

Raise the chalice and drink all the Precious Blood.
Do not take chalice from the mouth.
Do not throw head back.
Do not make a sucking noise.

(M.C. drops to his knees and prostrates himself. CHORUS continues to enact communion in an overtly sexual way. M.C. moans, in a tormented not a sexual way. Adverts at this stage must highlight the 'perfect' family. He then begins to kneel up. CHORUS lifts the ACOLYTE onto the altar. He takes a provocative pose, redolent of the crucifixion. CHORUS stands behind the altar. M.C. moves over to the altar drops to his knees and clings on to ACOLYTE'S feet. ACOLYTE mocks this act. CHORUS pulls ACOLYTE off the altar away from the M.C. and they move across to the armchair and television, where they then watch the adverts and begin to zap around the channels. M.C. is alone at the altar. ACOLYTE moves to the cubicle and turns television off with remote control. M.C. moves across to chair and he sits down as if continuing to watch the television. The CHORUS sits around the chairs, discordantly singing one of the most overtly family-oriented adverts. CHORUS then tips M.C. out of chair and removes television and chair. M.C. searches for remote control, watched by ACOLYTE who is standing in the doorway of the cubicle. ACOLYTE uses remote control on M.C. and as he is zapped; M.C. goes through a range of responses. In the following sections, insert snippets from adverts (sung to appropriate tune), juxtaposed to parts of the religious ceremony and snatches of conversation with WIFE and children.)

M.C.
[Advert]...Ceremonial kisses, Osculum. Occur frequently, made by touching the object with closed lips...[Advert]...The two persons stand facing each other with hands joined...McDonalds! Yeah, we'll take the kids to McDonalds...The one who is to receive the kiss bows. The one who is to receive it lays his hands on the shoulders of the other...You can't be too careful these days, come straight home...[Advert]...Bow the head forward so that the left cheeks...I'm sorry love I forgot it...of the two persons almost...Perverts...touch...shall I go and get

some?…*Pax Tecum*…
(*M.C. collapses, exhausted. Light fades.*)

Scene Five

(*Lights up to indicate toilet. ACOLYTE is standing in the same place as in previous scene. M.C. enters SL. CHORUS watch through grid.*
M.C. goes through the usual rituals of washing and drying his hands very carefully. He also goes to the table, takes a flower from the vase and puts it in his lapel.)

M.C.
Flowers on the altar should be used with great restraint. None are used in Rome but custom favours them in England and Ireland.

(*He then turns and looks at the ACOLYTE. As they are staring at each other, the CHORUS enters SL to music, all dressed as men. They surround the M.C. cutting him off from the ACOLYTE, who stands watching from the cubicle entrance. The CHORUS then dances suggestively around/with the M.C. The CHORUS should be as masculine as possible. The M.C. is drawn to them but desperately resists their advances. He tries to leave the toilet, but is pulled back by them. They mock and taunt him. He looks to the ACOLYTE for help, but the ACOLYTE just stands watching, mildly amused.*
The M.C. manages to break out from the toilet and into the supermarket. The difference between music, lighting and atmosphere is important. He is followed out of the toilet by the CHORUS who pursue him as he moves uneasily around the supermarket. The CHORUS is joined by the ACOLYTE who interacts with it. They ignore the M.C.. The M.C. begins following them and as they once more return to the toilet he now pursues them. The ACOLYTE watches. The M.C. is now submissive and is seduced by one of the CHORUS. As the M.C. begins to undress 'him' the rest of the CHORUS also begin to remove their masculine clothes. The M.C. begins to kiss and touch his partner. It is with utter disgust he realises 'he' is in fact with a woman and not as he supposed, a man. M.C. crosses to the basin and is sick. The CHORUS continues to mock the M.C. by acting in an overtly camp way. In his desperation the M.C. looks to the ACOLYTE for help. The ACOLYTE is standing in front of the altar, dancing 'the twist' provocatively. He indicates to the M.C. to join him, which he does. They both do a very stylised, sexual twist in front of the altar.)

Scene Six

(*ACOLYTE begins to question, tempt and taunt M.C..*)
ACOLYTE
Do you enjoy being homosexual?

M.C.
No…I'm not. Not really.

ACOLYTE
Why are you disgusted by women?

M.C.
I'm not.

ACOLYTE
Oh no?

M.C.
I like women. I'm married to one. But they don't belong in here.
I was tricked. I thought they were men…like us.

ACOLYTE
Like us? You and me you mean?
You think we're alike?

M.C.
They desecrate the place.
They are profane.

ACOLYTE
Who does disgust you then? Me?…No, you.
You disgust yourself don't you?
Why does a respectable married man need to sneak into the supermarket toilets
and rodger young men?
Because that's what you really like doing isn't it?
Why do it?
Does it feed your own feelings of guilt?
No…that's not enough is it?
It not only feeds your guilt, your guilt actually craves for it.
You could say you binge out on it.

M.C.
I can be absolved.
I seek solace in the confessional.

ACOLYTE
But the demons won't go, will they?
What if you were caught?

M.C.
I would be a public disgrace. Shunned and mocked…

ACOLYTE
…and martyred?
You've children? A boy…What would you do if you met your son in here one
day?
What would you do if your son was in here
Waiting…
Just like I stand in here waiting…
Like you stand in here waiting?
Think of what we do together,
In there
Just the two of us,
So close,
So intimate.
Imagine me and your son in there,
Together, close and intimate.

The Lusty Juventus production of Ceremonial Kisses, *December 1996.*
Photograph by Geraint Lewis.

M.C.
I'd kill you. I wouldn't let it happen...I'd kill you.

ACOLYTE
Ah. So public humiliation and public contempt is good enough for you but not for your flesh and blood.
The ecstasy you desire would be deprived from junior?
You can find forgiveness in the confessional,
But your son and I...
Wouldn't find it in you?

Tut tut. It is true then, you are a hypocrite. But I expect you can be absolved from that as well.
In the confessional...in the cubicle.

(The ACOLYTE leads M.C. into the cubicle.)

ACOLYTE
By the way, how old is your son?

M.C.
Fifteen.

ACOLYTE
Just the age you like them.

Scene Seven

(Lighting for church. M.C. leads ACOLYTE out of the cubicle.)

M.C.
Those who are about to celebrate the holy mysteries must have confessed their sins.

(Enter CHORUS in pairs and reverently perform the rituals as dictated by M.C..)
M.C.
Notice the inferior members walk in front of the elder or superior ones. The more dignified walk before the others. They walk in pairs and take the holy water. The one nearer the stoup giving it to the companion by dipping his own fingers and holding them towards the other, who touches them.
Now you.

ACOLYTE
But I'm not in the choir.

M.C.
No one enters the house of God until he takes the Holy Water.
Go on!

(ACOLYTE performs the ritual, but with little conviction.)

M.C.
Now make the sign of the cross.

(ACOLYTE makes the sign of the cross, incorrectly. As M.C. is explaining how it should be done, CHORUS does it in perfect synchrony. ACOLYTE is mildly amused.)

M.C.
No! Place the left hand extended under the breast.
Hold the right hand extended also.
At the words *Patris* raise it and touch forehead;
At *Filii* touch the breast at a sufficient distance down, but above the left hand;
At *Spiritus Sancti* touch the left and right shoulders,
At Amen join the hands.
Good.

Now?

ACOLYTE
I don't bloody know!

M.C.
Genuflect!

ACOLYTE
Oh fuck this.

(M.C. grabs ACOLYTE by the back of the neck as he begins to walk away.)

M.C.
To make a genuflection, without bending the body or the head,
Touch the ground with the right knee at exactly the place where the right foot was.
Rise again! At once.

(M.C. physically forces ACOLYTE to do this, whilst chorus do it with perfect timing.)

ACOLYTE
I love it when you play rrrough.

M.C.
Chorus good.
It is most important that any act should be performed by all,
Uniformly, together.
This means bowing, kneeling, and rising.

(CHORUS now goes to the altar and stands either side of it.)

Never stand either side of the altar…Ah ha! You forgot.

(CHORUS move to stand in a group.)

There are three voices in High Mass.
Vox Clara – clear voice sung aloud or a plain chant.
Voce Submissa – medium or subdued voice.
Voc Secreta – secret voice an articulated whisper.

Now try it. Let me see.

(CHORUS begins to sing, changing their voices as the M.C. dictates.)

M.C.
Vox Clara…Voce Submissa…Voc Secreta…Voce Submissa…Vox Clara…Voc Secreta…Vox Clara.
Excellent! You're in fine voice today.
(to ACOLYTE)
Good taste and considerable skill are needed in the Master of Ceremony who trains the boys.
It is essential to the smooth running of the ceremony to find the right balance between sloppiness and pretension; control and passion.
It is much desired that young men should, when possible, minister at the altar, instead of small boys.

ACOLYTE
Here we go. That's more like it things are beginning to look up. What's next?

M.C.
Washing the fingers.

ACOLYTE
Mmm…sounds promising.

M.C.
With joined hands now go to the Epistle (right) end of the altar.

(ACOLYTE does as instructed. M.C. carries out the acts he is describing. From here until the end of the ceremony, all acts become overtly sexual.)

Face me.
Now hold your hands over the dish so that I can pour water over the ends of thumb and forefinger of each hand. Now I take the towel and dry them.
In so doing I hold the hands, not over the altar, but outside and in front of it.
Lavabo Inter Inoccentes.
We bow our heads towards the cross.
To bow we bend the head and body, low.
The hands are kept joined before the breast.
Gloria Patri.
Repeat.

ACOLYTE *(gradually being drawn into the rhythm of the sexual ritual.)*
To bow we bend the head and body, low.
The hands are kept joined before the breast.
Gloria Patri.

M.C.
Very good.
Now we come to the middle with joined hands.
Sicut Erat.
We look up and then lower our eyes.
We lay our hands, joined on the altar.
We bow – moderately.
And silently say the prayer:
Suscipe, Sancta Trinitas.

ACOLYTE
Siscipe, Sancta Trinitas.

(M.C. and ACOLYTE are now at the centre of the altar. They turn to face each other.)

ACOLYTE
Followed by?

M.C.
The Kiss of Peace.
The two persons stand facing each other with hands joined.

The one who is to receive the kiss bows.
Then the one who gives it lays his hands on the shoulders of the other,
Holding them at the elbows.
Each bows the head forward,
So that the left cheeks of the two persons…
Almost touch.
The one who gives the kiss says
Pax Tecum.

The other one answers
Et Cum Spiritu Tuo…

ACOLYTE
Et Cum Spiritu Tuo…

M.C.
Excellent. Now you're getting it…
Then they withdraw…only a little.
They stand again with joined hands
Facing each other
And bow.
Followed by…Can you remember?

ACOLYTE
Ceremonial Kisses.

M.C.
That's right.

ACOLYTE
These occur frequently,
And should be made by
Touching the 'object' with the closed lips.
On taking anything from the celebrant
First kiss his hand,
Then whatever is taken…is kissed.

*(M.C. leads ACOLYTE to the altar where they stand facing the audience.
CHORUS now sing/chant details of the Consecration of the Bread and Wine.
M.C. and ACOLYTE move to the ritual. It is not a literal representation of the
ceremony but reflects their intimacy.)*

CHORUS
Holding the bread, before them, between thumb and forefinger, they say,
secretly, distinctly and attentively the words of Consecration.
Hoc Est Enim Corpus Meum.
Then they stand erect.
They genuflect.
Holding the Host with both hands over the altar.
They rise at once and hold up
The Blessed Sacrament, so that it may be seen by the people.
It is then lowered onto the Corporal.
They lay their hands on the altar and genuflect again.

Rising from the second genuflection they take the chalice in both hands.
They lift it a little above the altar and set it down again at once.

They say *Gratias Agens*,
And bow their heads.
They say *Bene-Dixit*,
And make the sign of the cross
Over the chalice
With the right hand
Keeping the thumb and forefinger always joined
And then the words of Consecration over the chalice
Attentively, continuously and secretly.

Hic Est Enim Calix Sanguinis Mei Novi Et Aeterni Testamenti Mysterium Fidei
Qui Pro Vobis Et Pro Multis Effundetur In Remissionem Peccatorum.

They set the chalice on the altar,
Stand erect
And say
Haec Quoties Cumque Fereritis In Mei Memoriam Facietis.

M.C.
You are ready for Communion.

(M.C. and ACOLYTE move to the front of the altar where the ACOLYTE
receives Communion.)
Bow your head and receive Communion.
Do not extend the tongue.
Break the Sacred Species against the roof of your mouth
Do not touch with the teeth.

Rise.
Drink the Precious Blood.
Keeping the chalice at the mouth
Do not make a sucking noise.

(As M.C. is giving ACOLYTE Communion his mood begins to change. M.C.
turns the ACOLYTE around so he is facing the audience. M.C. puts his arm
around his throat. CHORUS sings or makes a selection of abstracted tableaux
to music.)

M.C.
Now the blessed Transubstantiation.

ACOLYTE
Christ, what's coming next?

M.C.
Yes, very good…He is.
Transubstantiation.

Where the symbol becomes a reality.
Where the body of Christ no longer is symbolic.

ACOLYTE
What?

M.C.
Where we actually eat the flesh of Christ and drink his blood.

ACOLYTE
Wouldn't that make you a cannibal?

(M.C. begins to bite ACOLYTE'S neck. ACOLYTE thinks he's just being sexual.)

ACOLYTE
Mmm nice. Perhaps there's something to be said for it after all.
(M.C. takes knife from the altar and rests it on ACOLYTES neck.)

ACOLYTE
What are you doing?...Hey, hang on...stop it...fuck off. This is no joke.

M.C.
No of course it's no joke.
At last you understand.
To eat the Sacred Flesh,
And drink the Precious Blood.

ACOLYTE
But I'm not Christ!
For fuck's sake, where do you think you are?

(ACOLYTE struggles but the M.C.'s grip holds fast. The CHORUS sing. He cuts the neck with the knife and drinks the blood from his neck.)

M.C.
Sanguis Domini Nostri
Drink all the Precious Blood,
Not throwing back the head or
Making a sucking sound.

Transubstantiation.
The whole substance, changed.
Changed in virtue of their consecration
Into the body and blood of Christ.

For this moment in time, here is Christ.

(He releases ACOLYTE who slumps to the floor.)

M.C.
He honoured me with his lips, but his heart was far from me.

(M.C. kneels by ACOLYTE'S side. He lifts his head to kiss him, but slips back into his obsession with rituals.)

M.C.
No.
There can be no kisses.
At Mass for the dead certain rules must be observed.
The vestments are black.
The altar frontal should also be black.
There can be no kisses.
At masses for the dead all kisses are omitted.

Blessings for the moment of death may be given to those who die in manifest mortal sin.

Mass for the dead, certain special rules,
No music, prayers sung…how?
Incense not wanted until…?
Stop the singing! The singing should have stopped by now.
All kisses omitted.
There should be silence.

(M.C. becomes increasingly panicked. CHORUS gather around ACOLYTE. M.C. rushes to stoop to wash his hands.)

M.C. AND CHORUS
In cases of urgency and necessity,
In danger of death or purgatory
Absolution can be given, quickly, short form.

M.C.
I need absolution,
Punishments merited by my sins.

(ACOLYTE sits up and looks across at him.)

ACOLYTE
You're on your own I'm afraid.
There's no one there.

M.C.
What are you doing? You're dead.

29

Oh no. Don't come that.
Not the resurrection.

ACOLYTE
You don't think I'd be so obvious?
No...Martyrdom.
That's what I fancy.
Martyrdom.

(ACOLYTE is lifted in the air by the chorus in mock martyr pose.)

M.C.
You can't be a martyr.
You haven't done anything to deserve it.

ACOLYTE
Well I was killed. That's a start.

M.C.
It's not enough. You don't think that everyone who's been killed is a martyr do you?

ACOLYTE
Yes I do actually. But if that's not enough in your eyes...
In your god's eyes, how about this?
My murder was a direct result of my belief in individual freedom.
I took risks to further the cause of free expression
No matter what bent that may take.
There you go, I was a freedom fighter.

M.C.
Bollocks!

ACOLYTE
Sorry to turn you down,
But we icons have our images to think of.

M.C.
But what about me? What's to become of me?
I've made you what you are!

ACOLYTE
Well as there's no absolution available,
It's Purgatory, then hell I suppose.
Y'know – *Confutatus Maledictus*,
Consigned to flames of woe,
Fire which never dies,

Burning you forever.
Actually it should suit you very well,
Tormented for eternity.
But you don't need me to describe it.
You've been better instructed in the horrors of hell than me.

I'm just a martyr to the cause.

(CHORUS and ACOLYTE enact montage of bizarre scenes with religious overtones, to music or singing, and force the M.C. back into the cubicle. When he is inside the CHORUS and ACOLYTE crawl over and around it, and then go back inside with the M.C..)

M.C.
Mea Culpa, mea culpa, mea culpa, mea culpa…

(M.C. begins pushing walls but is trapped. He begins to scream, then pushes his face to the muslin. The CHORUS takes up the same image.)

(Slow fade to blackout.)

(The end.)

The Lusty Juventus production of Ceremonial Kisses, December 1996.
Photograph by Geraint Lewis.

Part Two

Shading the Crime:
Acting Hopelessness as an Act of Hope
By Christine Roberts and Roberta Mock

Paulo Freire, the Brazilian author of *Pedagogy of the Oppressed*, sums up the dilemma for many politically-committed theatre-makers when he writes, 'while I certainly cannot ignore hopelessness as a concrete entity, nor turn a blind eye to the historical, economic, and social reasons that explain that hopelessness – I do not understand human existence, and the struggle needed to improve it, apart from hope and dream' (Freire, 1994: 8).

Confronted with the knowledge of systematised brutality and motivated by the desire to promote awareness and the potential for change, political performance struggles to present dichotomy in an art form that traditionally encourages coherence and unity. As theatre-makers, we must display a situation that is fixed, and yet simultaneously expresses freedom of choice.

Shading the Crime was premiered by Lusty Juventus in January 1998, co-directed by the authors of this article. The play is set in a special police unit in an unnamed country where gender-specific torture is used to humiliate, control and exert power over female 'political prisoners'. This country has a healthy tourist industry, despite its human rights atrocities, and is also seeking to secure trade deals. The play explores the duplicity of Western countries when dealing with and selling torture equipment to regimes that they know to be involved in human rights abuses.

By highlighting the set patterns of recruitment that are used when torturers are employed, it also aims to dispel the myth that torturers are a small group of people who are 'born evil'. *Shading the Crime* uncomfortably implies that we are all potentially capable of both dehumanizing acts and dehumanisation under certain extreme circumstances, and that many people avoid voicing their objections to human rights abuse due to opportunities for financial reward, or because a country offers a desirable holiday destination. We mentally 'shade out the crime'.

This article will focus on inherent contradictions that had to be acknowledged and exploited at the heart of the production. The narrative conflict that manifests itself in the relationship between the quiet power of the female prisoners and the socially constructed violence of their male guards was echoed stylistically by exploring the contrast between 'objective' linguistic structures and subjective physicality. The company used movement, vocal representation, choreographed dance, and scripted text – simultaneously juxtaposing naturalism and expressionistic symbolism – to create an environment of heightened realism. Strategies for political efficacy were mirrored in the production's rehearsal process, during which the company was forced to balance their feelings of rage and shock with a protective immunity towards the play's subject matter.

The Lusty Juventus production of Shading the Crime, *January 1998.*
Photograph by Sarah Swainson.

Recognition and Resistance

> Algeria, Turkey, and Columbia all promise investigations into the persecutions of human rights defenders. Very little happens. In the gap between rhetoric and reality, courageous people continue to be threatened, yet their work is crucial in countries where standing up for human rights risks assassination or disappearance. They are the only voice left to tell the world what is happening. (Bell, 1997)

At a political conference in 1998, some delegates (mainly from Eastern Europe) questioned the 'right' of an English playwright and company to deal with the issues raised in *Shading the Crime*.[1] 'After all', they said, 'You've never been tortured'. This, of course, is quite true, and there are two ways in which we respond to such criticism. Firstly, and without wishing to trivialise in any way the experience of political prisoners who have endured horrendous ordeals, it is necessary to point out that theatre is a system of signifying representations. A cathartic response amongst audience members relies on identification with archetypal images and primal situations. As Elin Diamond has observed in connection with the work of Caryl Churchill, 'the mystification of the body in representation has come to serve as a metaphor for the concealments of human, and especially female, experience under patriarchy and capitalism' (1997: 85). Like Churchill, by making explicit how the female body has been manipulated for the purposes of social control and maintained order, Lusty Juventus hoped to tap into a subconscious understanding of an experience which, at least in 'civilized' Western countries, seems deceptively remote.

Secondly, we in no way wish to 'replace' the first-hand accounts of dissidents who, unlike us, risk their lives and the safety of their families by attempting to inform a world-wide audience of their situations. This is what *Shading the Crime* is *about*; it is not a documentary, but a piece of art which asks people to reflect on the implications cloaked behind their daily mass-media bombardment of words and images, as well as their daily activities as consumers. The aim of the play is to provoke an audience to question, in Freire's words, 'the inevitability of the oppressive status-quo' (1994: 8). We wanted to present an audience with a realistic depiction of torture and brutality, of abuses of power, of manipulation and indifference. At the same time, however, it was important to portray a situation they could both identify with, and feel was possible to change. If the audience viewed the situation as hopeless, we would be failing in our aim of using political theatre to mobilise an audience into direct action, however limited in its scope.

For Boal and Brecht, oppressive ideology and the passivity of traditional theatre work in tandem. In their opinions, the manipulative ideologies of dominant cultures mean that the audience is not allowed to think for itself, and its 'passive position as spectators means it is not allowed to act for itself' (Fortier, 1997: 140). We too wish to make theatre that refuses to embed political expediency into its very practice and product while, in this case, rejecting the direct participation of Boal's 'spectators' or the full extent of Brechtian *Verfremdungseffekt* (though this, of course, does not preclude all forms of 'identification' by the spectators). Instead, we aimed for a delicate balance that both engaged and critically distanced our audience. As playwright Phyllis Nagy has said:

> What isn't valid is the overtly pedantic political play, when people walk into the theatre and know they're going to see, say, a Conservative leader fall from grace. The age has become far too cynical for that, tabloid coverage has become too good, no image is shocking. What needs to happen is for the play form to evolve to discourage pedantry and encourage popular participation. (qtd. in Bayley, 1995)

For spectators to react to the play's message, they must first be moved by its content. It seems that here we were successful. According to one critic, 'This was "in your face" theatre which had audience members sobbing and gasping with horror' (Old, 1998).

All of the torture practices in *Shading the Crime* are based on fact, and it was important for the audience to be confronted unequivocally with these facts. The reality of the situation on stage needed to prevent audience members from using the excuse that they were merely watching a fiction. It is for this reason that explicit depictions of torture were included in the production. The torture illustrates the gradual dehumanisation – not only of the three female prisoners – but also of the New Recruit, who is initiated into its acceptability. It also confirms both the vulnerability of the women and, at the same time, highlights their power and defiance. The torture scenes – which included: kicking;[2] punching;[3] sensory deprivation; suspending a menstruating woman upside down; urinating into a prisoner's mouth, and forcing her to perform oral sex on the New Recruit – are intrinsic to both the narrative action and theatrical approach of the play. We therefore hoped to avoid any accusation of being merely gratuitous.

Lusty Juventus, as a company, does not believe in hermetic aesthetics. As John Peter wrote in *The Sunday Times*: 'It is good for people to be shocked occasionally; more than good, it is essential...A cloistered and sequestered virtue ends up making up its own rules, and they usually exclude the idea that other people might be getting an unfair deal' (Peter, 1995).

For an audience to be sufficiently moved to act upon what they see, however, requires an intellectual response as well as an emotional one. The facts are woven around a fiction, a human story to which they could personally relate. In this way we hoped, in Raymond Williams' words, to, 'make hope practical, rather than despair convincing' (1983: 240). The situation needed to be believable, yet not hopeless. Audience members must understand the potential political efficacy, however limited, of the actions which they are motivated to take as a result of seeing the performance – i.e. refusing to holiday in, or buy products from, countries which engage in human rights abuse, or making a donation to an organisation like Amnesty International. Part of this understanding must also include an acknowledgement that there are no 'absolutes', no essential divisions between 'good' and 'evil'. The characters, regimes on which they are factually based, and we (as theatre-makers and audience members) are equally responsible for the stage action, its implications, and its consequences.

The narrative opens showing the Captain and his Officer selecting a range of torture equipment from a catalogue, and then moves to an isolation cell where Prisoner 3 is chained and blindfolded. Embossed on her leg-irons is the name of the English city in which they were manufactured. This is all based on fact,[4] and ensures that the international link is both a governmental and personal one.[5] Likewise, we see the manipulation of the characters working on a variety of levels: the Captain must satisfy his superior that his prison is suitable for an international visit in order to boost his own social status; the violence enacted upon the female prisoner is necessary to exert pressure on the male members of her family.[6] The play's narrative mainly focuses on the induction of the New Recruit, whose gradual dehumanisation mirrors that of the bewildered Prisoner 3. By learning how to treat her as an object, he is objectifying himself. This young man is not 'evil'; he is poor and unemployed. Like most 'trainee' torturers, he is gradually introduced to the brutality of systematised violence together with its own self-justifying logic and is then implicated, first by bearing witness to it, and then by direct action himself.

The final image of *Shading the Crime* ironically derives from the project's point of origin. A one-paragraph newspaper article, filed by Reuters and appearing as an 'In Brief' side panel in *The Guardian*, was spotted by both of us independently in 1996: eleven inmates on hunger strike in an El Salvadorian prison sewed up their mouths to show they were not eating. No other contextual information was given; nor was there any follow-up detailing the political efficacy of the prisoners' actions, nor even whether they died as a result of it. Presumably, the purpose of this extreme statement written on their very bodies *was* the short, easily missed article which we both read. The play, both in its intent as a piece of theatre and in its thematic content, mirrors the ambiguity of the strategy behind the image of the inmates' stitched lips.

After refusing to sign a confession to exonerate the prison authorities, Prisoner 1 is forced to swallow both the urine and semen of the young man who *may* be the son kidnapped from her as a baby by the government.[7] Following this degradation, she reinforces the optimism and integrity which she has displayed throughout the entire play, when urging her fellow prisoners to help her to sew her lips together:

> PRISONER 1
> I'll make sure no one ever forgets my face.
> You must help me, I can't do it alone.

She is requesting the aid of both the other women on stage, as well as the people watching in the audience. Problems immediately arise: there is no definitive proof that there will be an international visitor to the prison, and even if there is a visit, there is no guarantee when it will be. Prisoner 1 could die before this time, or else not be shown at all to the delegation. As Prisoner 2 articulates:

> PRISONER 2
> Plenty of other people have died at their hands, and they've gotten away with it. They just lie, and people are all too willing to accept their lies.

Finally, each audience member must decide what to *do* with the information with which s/he has been presented. Claire Bayley, concluding her article on (predominantly female) contemporary British theatre-makers, observes:

Playwrights can no longer offer certainties and nor do they want to.
Conflict is there, character is strong, even narrative is back in fashion, but
the sum of it all is a proliferation of questions and no answers. (Bayley,
1995)

While resistance may follow recognition, for both the characters in the play and
the audience watching it, the efficacy of resulting actions is not guaranteed.

It is in Prisoner 1's final gesture that the two seemingly contradictory functions
raised at the beginning of this article collide – that is, 'intellectual' theatre as a
political tool to raise consciousness, and 'emotional' theatre as an aesthetic art
object. The projected images of Prisoner 1's scars (if she indeed survives) will
forward the extra-narrative political debates that continue after the performance.
However, the motif of sealing off her mouth, the orifice which has been
violated, is a defiant refusal to comply with *any* form of oppressive ideology,
especially those which are rooted in patriarchal, class-based capitalism. Theatre,
at its most effective, is a place set apart for both personal and public
transformation. Foucault refers to it as heterotopia, 'a quasi-public space which
functions to reflect, expose, invert, support or compensate for the outside world'
(1986: 24–7).

Theatre of Catastrophe

Within the framework of this 'quasi-public space', it is most often the function
of characterisation to provoke and provide opportunities for moral reflection
within the *mise en scène*. Tim Etchells, of Forced Entertainment, has identified
why the re-presentation of character as mediator of audience response is
difficult now that, in McLuhan's words, 'the medium is the message': 'We're so
haunted by other versions of ourselves and our lives as reflected by the media
that it comes to us second-hand, and that fundamentally affects our notion of
character. It means you can't present a character that can speak with a single
voice, but only a collection of eyes or voices which circulate around a fixed
point' (qtd. in Bayley, 1995).

Characters thus represent a confluence of social, political, and historical
influences and experiences, rather than reified point of view. It is not who a
character is, but what s/he does, which is used to situate him or her within a
socio-political (and thereby, theatrical) context. Audience identification is
therefore defined, not by the role, but by the way in which the character
searches for that role.

The characters in *Shading the Crime* have no names, nor any definitive detailed
histories. Their pasts are a collection of selective events. What is emphasised is
not how they think, but how they are responding, and these responses are
consistent with their previous actions, both within the narrative and as theatrical
devises. The perception each character has of his/her own self-identity is

inextricably linked to political and performative purposes, which embody moral imperatives. Howard Barker, in setting out his theory of a Theatre of Catastrophe, locates dramatic tension as, 'derived from the contradictory currents felt when wrong actions are passionately performed in pursuit of self-consciousness' (1989: 59). Prisoner 1's actions, like Katrin's in Barker's *The Europeans*, are 'impossible to assimilate'; they reveal the 'annihilation of individual pain in collective orthodoxy'. These 'wrong actions' which cause disturbance, anxiety, and moral consideration, are also 'moments of beauty' which signify freedom: 'If a theatre of Catastrophe takes as its material the individual and the individual's ability to effect self-identification in a collective or historical nightmare, the moment of beauty is the moment of collision between two wills, the will of the irrational protagonist (the non-ideological) and the will of the irrational state (the officially ideological)' (Barker, 1989: 61).

While part of Prisoner 1's motivation for sewing her lips together is certainly an ideological gesture of collective protest on behalf of all political prisoners, it is also an irrational and idealistic act of defiance by a rape victim. This 'irrationality' and 'wrongness' is signified by the acknowledged ambiguity of the action's potential efficacy. Though Barker stresses the need to treat an audience not as a collective, but as a collection of individuals, we still believe in the possibility of a nearly-uniform acknowledgement among audience members that a situation is 'immoral', and that this is only possible when presented with irrefutable 'truth' on stage. We do not see this condition as being incompatible with Barker's general aim: 'The artist's response to the primacy of fact must be to revive the concept of knowledge, which is a private acquisition of an audience thinking individually and not collectively, an audience isolated in darkness and stretched to the limits of tolerance.' (Barker, 1989: 50). Ultimately, the purpose of displaying obscenity and violence is to return the responsibility for moral argument and choice of resulting action back to the audience itself.

There are, however, many differences between our outlook and that of Barker. Looking at his distinctions between Humanist and Catastrophic Theatre, for example (1989: 91), it is obvious that several of our principles fall into the reviled camp and that, most probably, only Howard Barker could make theatre which specifically follows Howard Barker's theories. We use his ideas here to both illuminate our practice and to locate our work within a theatrical context. However, Lusty Juventus are not slaves to theory, nor do we follow any deliberate manifesto that dictates how theatre should be presented. What is clear to us is that, in order to make theatre which induces an audience to both feel and think, this strategy must be embedded into its very stagecraft as well as its narrative content. As words, on their own, have a tendency to replicate the structures of dominant ideologies – and in the play the words of the guards are particularly manipulative, often dishonest, and always a product of social conditioning – coupled with the fact that we wish to avoid overt didacticism in our theatre, we often use expressionistic movement and sound to highlight what may be deemed abstract (e.g. tensions in relationships or within the individual characters, desire, responsibility, fear, status, etc.).

These elements within the play are never discrete; physical and vocal symbolism is always used to comment on, and inform, dialogic content. In *Shading the Crime*, all performers were on stage for the entire play, in constant view. The set was designed to simulate a panopticon, with the prisoners' main cell and isolation cell downstage and guards' office upstage, separated by barbed wire and enclosed from above by a version of playground equipment. The prisoners could always be seen by their guards but, more importantly, the way the guards and the prisoners reflected each other could be seen in totality by the audience (and the audience could be seen in totality by the actors). It was the guards who were usually seen as if in a cage; the prisoners' cells were open to the audience. This means that, for example, while the Captain was explaining to the New Recruit that many female dissidents abandoned their children, Prisoner 1 performed a dance – both for herself and her audience – reflecting her anger, frustration and panic as her son was kidnapped, while the Officer climbed over the top of the set's frame like a barely controlled animal. This use of space encompasses the possibility of representations that are simultaneously private and public, personal and shared, literal and symbolic.

We describe Lusty Juventus as a politically committed text-based physical theatre company. Due to a puzzling need to label types of performance for public consumption, many people would choose to describe our approach as 'Total Theatre'. The term, used most generally, is an appropriate description of the 'style' (or anti-style) employed in *Shading the Crime*. Peter Brook describes it as, 'the time-honoured notion of getting all the elements of the stage to serve the play'. Total Theatre is, 'the jangle produced by the clash of styles' in which 'everything' – intellectual ideas, sensory experiences and physical images – is put in its place by its neighbour; 'abstraction is vivified by the stage image, the violence illuminated by the cool flow of thought' (Brook, 1995: 6). However, in attempting to establish a balance between 'abstraction' and 'the cool flow of thought', we uncover the problems inherent in Total Theatre as a generic term, in strategies for using this 'style' as a political tool, and specifically in the coherence of our production as an art object.

Our production process revealed that Total Theatre can derive from two different historical lineages, and this is reflected not so much in the nature of theatrical materials included in a production, but in the effect of the weighting given to them. It would be naïve to suggest that as directors we share an identical artistic viewpoint; in fact, one of the reasons we have chosen to work together is because we do not, and this tension, when harnessed toward a common goal, can enrich a production. Roberta Mock's main influences in the creation of Total Theatre are Jean-Louis Barrault and Peter Brook. Their work is closely connected in many respects (on a practical level, Barrault asked Brook to direct the Centre for International Theatre Research in 1968), especially in their Artaudian emphasis on sensuality, spectacle, physical affirmation, ritual, primitivism, and the projection of internal landscapes. However, as Christopher

Innes (1993) has pointed out, even when those practitioners were dealing with ostensibly 'political' material (like *Rabelais* or the *Marat/Sade*), each had a tendency to subjugate rational dialectic by stressing aestheticism. This effect would, obviously, be inappropriate for *Shading the Crime*. As such, our strategy became one in which the sum of these elements contributed to an overall form of Total Theatre more closely associated with Erwin Piscator, with which Christine Roberts identifies as both director and playwright.

For Piscator, the notion of 'totality' was necessarily linked to two other concepts: immediacy and authenticity. Immediacy meant that the play should be linked to current events, and authenticity meant that it should be soundly based in a socio-political reality. To achieve these aims, Piscator drew on a range of techniques in order to juxtapose fact and drama: 'I know of no means that can be termed inartistic so long as it communicates a spirit of movement, tension, expression, in other words – of life' (qtd. in Willet, 1978: 113). In *Shading the Crime*, we employed many of Piscator's techniques: song and dance to present a message in 'the simplest way'; fluidity and force of expression to assault the senses; music to show subconscious thought. The latter was particularly effective in the case of the New Recruit, whose guitar playing was first used to indicate his youth and freedom of creative expression, and then his indoctrination as the guitar was handled like a gun in a military drill, thumping out an angry, codified rhythm.

The Lusty Juventus production of Shading the Crime, *January 1998.*
Photograph by Sarah Swainson.

Piscator wanted his Total Theatre to immerse the audience in the action of the piece, using texts, speeches or situations that the audience knew were drawn from real events. While we did not use slides or documentary film, the audience was clearly informed of the authenticity of the torture practices in the play through programme notes and indirectly through the production's link with Amnesty International. Finally, Piscator wished to portray a complex picture within the time available, through swiftness of communication and the speed of scene changes. *Shading the Crime* was one continuous action which was not interrupted by curtains or intervals, the scenes interlocked through the cross-fading of lighting states, and action in all stage areas was maintained even when it was not the narrative focus. Piscator intended the use of music, sound, and movement to make his performances universal, 'expanding them in time, space, and meaning', as *Shading the Crime* revealed there is a balance to be found between a literal authentic level and the symbolism of resistance to less specific forms of oppression.

Piscator's concept of Total Theatre also included 'objective acting', whereby the actors should use whatever performance technique necessary to show their character's class or political function. It is at this point – defining the function of character – that contradictory strands in the conceptual framework of Total Theatre became problematic in both the process and product of *Shading the Crime*. While all the other theatrical elements were intended to serve one single function, which contributed to a 'total' hyper-real *mise en scène*, the actors were asked to embody all functions, literal and symbolic, within their individual characterizations. According to Barrault: 'As soon as there is, on four raised planks, no matter where, a man *(sic)*, and nothing around him, expressing himself in the whole range of his means of expression, there will be…total theatre' (qtd. in Innes, 1993: 104).

In short, the actor needed to represent his/her political function while simultaneously exhibiting the impetus towards, and manifestations of, individuality; s/he needed to do this subjectively and objectively, in actuality and illusion, as fact and fiction, physically and verbally. The actors needed to embody the very contradictions at the centre of the production, and this proved unsuccessful for two reasons: firstly, it cluttered the over-arching strategy for the production as a whole; secondly, due primarily to casting problems, the actors did not have time to fully explore the inter-relation between the forms and content of their expression.

This exploratory process was necessarily painful due to the subject matter and content of the play. Early rehearsals were spent engaging in actions without fully understanding what enabled them or how they were to be emotionally resolved. It was not too difficult to eventually devise ways of representing 'objective' political functioning, or to justify a character's actions using these tools (the emphasis of Piscator's 'Total Theatre'). What was more challenging was to develop an understanding of the actions on an individual interior plane, and to deal with the resulting relationship between actor and character (the emphasis of Barrault's 'Total Theatre'). As Boal has pointed out, 'memory and imagination form part of the same psychic process: one does not exist without the other' (Boal, 1995: 21). For many of us, confronting the issues in the play meant confronting the memory of past abuses of power. It meant having either to recall being the victim of, or to imagine oneself capable of, extreme violence. For Ruth Way, who choreographed the production and played Prisoner 1, re-enacting humiliation and self-immolation every night was traumatic. During the rehearsal period, when there was constant communication between cast members, this trauma was less acute than during the London run when she felt very isolated with her character and needed 'irrational' reassurance, especially from the male actors, that they were not capable of the thoughts and actions of their characters. The reconciliation between objective and subjective acting technique, necessary to produce a performance that the audience could both empathise with, and critically distance themselves from, became unravelled in a less supportive environment.

As a result of these experiences, it was necessary for each of us to develop a self-protective immunity. At a certain point, we needed to stop being enraged, shocked, disgusted and frightened by the actions of the play. For each person this happened at a different time, depending on his or her role in the production: for Christine Roberts it was during the writing of the play; for Roberta Mock it was during the formation of a production strategy; for the actors it was during rehearsals. It was this distancing which allowed us to incorporate much of our ambivalence toward the project into the production. Many of us were disturbed to discover that we found aspects of the torture scenes in the play sexually stimulating, despite being fully aware of their context. This suggested fears that the play had the potential of being viewed voyeuristically, and reinforced the necessity of integrity and authenticity. We questioned our motivation for creating violent imagery and whether we were being gratuitous or sensational. Finally, it was decided that, rather than pretend that people are not attracted to dark events and situations, we would stress instead the relationship between this attraction and our social conditioning which has produced it. As Edward Bond has said, 'People who do not want writers to write about violence want to stop them writing about our time and us. It would be immoral not to write about violence' (Bond, 1978: 3).

After a performance, when audience members visibly disturbed by what they saw in *Shading the Crime* wondered how we could calmly stand beside them at the bar and order drinks, it was because they hadn't stopped 'feeling' the play and had begun to 'think' about it. They, like us, had to disentangle fact and fiction, intellect and emotion, from their reading of the play. Like Barker, we believe that theatre primarily 'must locate its creative tension not between characters and arguments on the stage but between the audience and the stage itself' (Barker, 1989: 52). We have provided no certitudes, only complexity, pain, and the possibility of reconstruction. And hope.

Notes

[1] 'Whatever Happened to Political Theatre?' conference. Theatre Museum & Goldsmith's College, London. 2–3 May 1998.

[2] Common torture inflicted on organisers of peaceful demonstrations in China include severe beatings, and the application of high voltage shocks to head, neck, shoulders, armpits, stomach and between the legs. When electroshock batons run out of power, prison guards resort to kicking the prisoners. (Source: Amnesty International)

[3] Gulbahar Gunduz was accused of belonging to an illegal Marxist party. Turkish policemen blindfolded her, put a gun to her neck and threatened to kill her. They stripped her and aimed cold water jets at sensitive parts of her body. They applied electric shocks to her toes and ears. Her torturers then beat her till she was hospitalised. When she was admitted to hospital, staff had to stop her police guards from beating her in her hospital bed. She was acquitted by a Turkish court of belonging to an illegal party, but one year after her arrest she was still confined to a wheelchair. (Source: Amnesty International)

[4] 'I was held for almost a month in leg-irons that had been imported from Sheffield, England. My legs swelled. I was incommunicado from my family and friends'. (Shakafwa Chihana, POC, Malawi)

[5] The United Kingdom boasts the second-biggest arms exports in the world. Small arms cause ninety per cent of war casualties. Eighty-four per cent of the murdered and maimed are ordinary men and women, almost half are children. (Source: *The Guardian*, 15 June 1998)

[6] Amal is twenty-eight-years-old and one of many Egyptian women taken hostage and tortured by the authorities to collect evidence against men in their families, who are suspected Muslim militants. 'They whipped me with cable wire, kicked me in the stomach and sliced open my back with razors. This lasted two hours. I could hear my husband screaming'. (Source: *The Observer*, 22 September 1996)

[7] Four years after the end of El Salvador's civil war, the country began to discover the truth about what happened to hundreds of its lost children: they were seized from villages by the American-backed military and falsely written off as war orphans, even as relatives spent years searching for them or clinging to the hope that they were safe. Many were abducted by soldiers as part of a wider practice of removing children from battlefields, sometimes from their mother's arms. (Source: *The Guardian*, 20 July 1996). In *Shading the Crime*, the New Recruit is manipulated into humiliating Prisoner 1 as an attempt to distance himself from his potential origins.

Works Cited

Barker, H. (1989) *Arguments for a Theatre*. London: John Calder.

Bayley, C. (1995) 'Playwrights Unplugged', *The Independent*, 24 February.

Bell, M. (1997) *Human Rights, Human Wrongs*. BBC2, broadcast 9 December.

Boal, A. (1995) *The Rainbow of Desire*. London: Routledge.

Bond, E. (1978) *Plays: Two*. London: Methuen.

Brook, P. (1995) Introduction to Weiss, *Marat/Sade*. London: Marion Boyars.
Diamond, E. (1997) *Unmaking Mimesis*. London: Routledge.

Fortier, M. (1997) *Theory/Theatre*. London: Routledge.

Foucault, M. (1986) 'Of Other Spaces', *Diacritics*, 16.1.

Freire, P. (1994) *Pedagogy of Hope: Reliving Pedagogy of the Oppressed*. New York: Continuum.

Innes, C. (1993) *Avant Garde Theatre 1892-1992*. London: Routledge.

Old, N. (1998) 'Brave Performances Tell Tales of Torture', *Express & Echo* (Exeter), 15 January.

Peter, J. (1995) 'Alive When Kicking', *The Sunday Times*, 29 January.

Willet, J. (1978) *The Theatre of Erwin Piscator*. London: Methuen.

Williams, R. (1983) *Towards 2000*. London: Chatto & Windus.

Shading the Crime

Shading the Crime was premiered by Lusty Juventus on 12 January 1998 at the New Theatre, Exeter, with the following cast: James Barlow (New Recruit); Lara Fergus (Prisoner 2); Mark McGarvey (Officer); Mark Shorto (Captain); Ruth Way (Prisoner 1) and Kelly Wright (Prisoner 3).

Co-directed by Roberta Mock and Christine Roberts. Choreography by Ruth Way. Set design by Russell Frampton. Lighting design by Cyril Squire. Props/costumes by Sam Shaw. Sound design by Rube. The production transferred to the Hackney Empire Studio Theatre, London, 14–17 January 1998, and the Man in the Moon Theatre, London, 22-31 January 1998.

The Courtyard Production

Shading the Crime was chosen from over four hundred scripts as the inaugural play at the Courtyard Theatre, Hereford. It opened on 6 October 1998 with the following cast: Lynette Clarke (Prisoner 1); Kenneth Collard (Officer); Nick Ellsworth (Captain); Mark Lawrence (New Recruit); Lyndsay Maples (Prisoner 2) and Mary McNally (Prisoner 3).
Directed by Ellie Parker. Design by Bruno Santini.

The Characters

Captain (a married man in his early sixties with adult children and two grandchildren)
Officer (a married man in his forties with teenage children)
New Recruit (a seventeen-year-old, engaged to be married)
Prisoner 1 (a married mother in her forties)
Prisoner 2 (a single woman in her mid-late twenties with no children)
Prisoner 3 (a seventeen-year-old woman)

Act One

Scene One

(Area lit Stage Right (SR). The Captain's Office. There are two uniformed men: the CAPTAIN is sitting at his desk, reading from a pile of sales promotional brochures, the OFFICER sits on another chair. He is preoccupied with cutting things out and sticking them in a scrapbook.)

OFFICER
When does the order have to be in?

CAPTAIN
End of this week.

OFFICER
How much've you got to spend?

CAPTAIN
A few thousand.

OFFICER
Waste of money if you ask me…

CAPTAIN
How about this? Stun belts, from Sten-Tech Inc., allows officers to inflict
severe pain and incapacitate a prisoner at the push of a button.
(The CAPTAIN reads from pamphlet.)
"If you were wearing a contraption around your waist that, by the merest push
of a button in someone else's hand, could make you defecate or urinate yourself,
where would you stand from the psychological standpoint?" It says it gives an
eight-second fifty thousand volt shock. Sounds good, and it's used by the US
government. *(Continues reading from pamphlet.)* "No medical evidence to
show they are either dangerous or cruel."

OFFICER
Waste of money…

CAPTAIN
Or this one. "Black Rod". *(Reads from different pamphlet.)* "Electro-shock
weapons," sold to China and Indonesia. "Very easy for under-trained guards to
use. Particularly good to psychologically threaten, inflict pain and incapacitate
people". Well? What do you suggest?

OFFICER
I've told you I think it's a waste of money. Could be useful for the new recruit I
suppose. What time's his interview?

CAPTAIN
Midday. You think he'll be good?

OFFICER
He has potential.

CAPTAIN
You're sure about the family?

OFFICER
Certain.

CAPTAIN
Good. I've got to buy something; otherwise they'll cut my budget.

OFFICER
Look, get a few belts, and a couple of rods. But I still think the clamps we use are just as good. All this new stuff. They're just jumping on the bandwagon. At least ours are locally made.

CAPTAIN
British company though…

OFFICER
Still brings employment…that factory employs two hundred local people. My oldest boy's just got a job there. They can think about starting a family now. Just think I could be a grandfather this time next year.

CAPTAIN
There's nothing like it. You know I think I've enjoyed the grandchildren more than my own children. Never thought I'd say it.

OFFICER
You should be proud, they're great kids. Bloody strike could put a halt to my boy's plans though…fucking communist militants…what time are you returning the isolate to the main cell?

CAPTAIN
There's no hurry.

OFFICER
No…let her stew. She'll be even more grateful then.

CAPTAIN
But be careful with her, we don't want the numbers to fall too low. It could reflect badly on us, make us look careless in our practises.

OFFICER
How did you explain the last one?

CAPTAIN
I told them she'd eaten something 'incompatible with her health'.

OFFICER
Excellent. And the doctor?

CAPTAIN
No problem. He verified it.

OFFICER
Coffee?

(Light fades.)

Scene Two

(Lights up on small, bare area Stage Left (SL). The Isolation Cell. One woman is bound by leg-irons and blindfolded. She is feeling some writing embossed on the leg-irons.)

PRISONER 3
What are these letters? These letters…on the leg-irons?…No one has come yet…So why do they keep me in here?…There is no air or ventilation. Is it their intention that I suffocate? It must be. That's why I am removed from the main cell. They want me to suffocate so they can tell my family I died of natural causes. With no marks on my body, proof for the world that they did not touch me…I must stay calm, not use up the air with my panic…
S…H…E…F…F…I…E…L…D. Sheffield? Where is Sheffield I wonder? I wonder where it is? What are the people who live in Sheffield doing this very second? What is this very second? What is the person doing who made these irons, at this very moment…Now? Did he know? Was he forced? How else could he make them? What did he think they would be used for?…Or was it a woman? A woman like me? Is she married like me? Does she have children like mine? S…H…E…F…F…I….E…L…D…Sheffield. Who made them? Why am I here? Am I here? I am here. Here I am…Why?

Scene Three

(Captain's office. CAPTAIN is in his chair still looking at the brochures. OFFICER brings in the new recruit.)

OFFICER
Here he is.

CAPTAIN
Young isn't he? Or are we just getting older?

OFFICER
I like to think of it as more experienced.

CAPTAIN
Well we can be sure he's lacking that. How old are you?

RECRUIT
Seventeen sir.

CAPTAIN
Sit down and make yourself comfortable. Is this the first job you've been interviewed for?

RECRUIT
Thank you sir, no sir.

CAPTAIN
Tell me what you've already applied for.

RECRUIT
I've applied to the factory and some offices.

CAPTAIN
No luck?

RECRUIT
No sir. I lacked experience, and with many people wanting work I didn't stand a chance.

CAPTAIN
Do you have experience in our line of work?

RECRUIT
No sir, but I am very willing to learn.

CAPTAIN
Good. Actually we prefer people to start without experience. Ours, you see, is specialised work. Craftsmen – that's what we see ourselves as. People are admired for taking a pride in their work – take a carpenter or a sculptor. Our work is not so different…Nothing we like better than turning a piece of wood, and we're pretty good with the hammer and chisel – chipping away here and there until we achieve the desired results. And we like it done our way. Isn't that right Officer?

OFFICER
Absolutely.

CAPTAIN
You presumably know what we do here?

RECRUIT
Yes sir. The Officer explained it to me.

CAPTAIN
Tell me, what do we do?

RECRUIT
You ensure the smooth running of the country, and support for the government.

CAPTAIN
That's the sort of work which interests you then is it?

RECRUIT
Of course sir.

CAPTAIN
Why?

RECRUIT
Well we need a law-abiding atmosphere so we can lead decent lives. I intend to get married and have children, sir, and I don't want them brought up with war and trouble all round.

CAPTAIN
Do you remember the war or, should I say, the rebellion?

RECRUIT
No sir, I was only a baby at the time, but my parents have talked about it to me.

CAPTAIN
What have they told you?

RECRUIT
That there was a great shortage of food and essentials, and that the country was in complete disarray. People were victimised for being successful and making something of themselves. My parents were attacked for just wanting to better themselves and to lead a decent life. They have worked very hard for what they have, why should someone come along and tell them they have no right to it.

CAPTAIN
You think highly of your parents?

RECRUIT
Of course sir, we should respect our parents. They have done everything for me. I now hope to repay them by making them proud of me.

CAPTAIN
You think they'll be proud of you if you join us?

RECRUIT
Of course, they support the government and so do I. It has been very good to us.

CAPTAIN
And girlfriends, do you have a special girlfriend?

RECRUIT
Yes sir.

CAPTAIN
Tell me about her. Is she pretty? I'm sure she must be.

RECRUIT
Yes sir, she is very pretty and kind. But that doesn't mean she's not intelligent. She might be going to college.

CAPTAIN
Of course. Do you have a photograph?

RECRUIT
Yes sir, would you like to see it? Here, this was taken at my parents' house…on my birthday.

CAPTAIN
Mmm, indeed she is pretty, and your parents look most respectable. Don't you think so? *(Hands the OFFICER the photograph.)*

OFFICER
A fine family, no wonder you're proud.

RECRUIT
I am sir. My girlfriend and I plan to marry as soon as we have saved enough money.

CAPTAIN
You have answered very well, and truthfully. I think you will fit in here. We can offer you a position. But you understand that we run things as strictly as an army. You take orders from my Officer, but everyone here answers to me. You understand?

RECRUIT
Yes sir.

CAPTAIN
You are ready to start tomorrow? Good, your training will begin then. Make

sure you tell your family that you will be staying here with us during your training.

RECRUIT
Thank you sir, I won't let you down. I appreciate very much the opportunity you are giving me. How long will my training be sir?

CAPTAIN
As long as it takes boy, as long as it takes. That's not a problem is it?

RECRUIT
No. Of course not sir. I'll let them know not to expect me until they see me sir. Thank you sir, thank you.

CAPTAIN
Enough, enough…on your way.

(RECRUIT is escorted out by the OFFICER. The RECRUIT is clearly delighted.)

Scene Four

(Area lit Centre-stage. The Main Cell. There are two women.)

PRISONER 1
There must be a visit due.

PRISONER 2
Why?

PRISONER 1
Haven't you noticed we're getting more food? It won't last long though…but it could be good news. It could mean they set us free before the visitors arrive, or we get a chance to put our case. To speak out.

PRISONER 2
I doubt it. Look where speaking out has got us.

PRISONER 1
It's not quite that simple, as you well know.

PRISONER 2
No I know, of course I know. But your continued optimism bloody irritates me. Why can't you be normal and be depressed?

PRISONER 1
Because it's so negative. It clouds the mind and makes you more susceptible to the humiliation. If someone is going to visit us I want to make sure we take advantage of it.

PRISONER 2
Have you heard anything from the new prisoner?

PRISONER 1
Nothing at all. They must be trying to weaken her first.

PRISONER 2
Do you know anything about her?

PRISONER 1
No, not that I'm aware of anyway.

PRISONER 2
Why have they got her then?

PRISONER 1
There you go again, looking for logic. You should know yourself that refusing to leave your own village is enough to bring you here, if you're lucky enough not to be shot first. At least ours was deliberate action...If they don't release us, where will they put us when he comes?

PRISONER 2
He who?

PRISONER 1
The visitor.

PRISONER 2
How do you know it will be a man?

PRISONER 1
It usually is.

PRISONER 2
You don't even know if there is going to be a visit.

PRISONER 1
I know, not for sure anyway. But they always begin to feed us up when they feel threatened. We don't want to be caught unawares.

PRISONER 2
You do this all the time, don't you?

PRISONER 1
Of course. I know myself; I know why I behave like this. If this place does nothing else at least you come to know your own nature. We always thought we'd be prepared if we were caught, we tried to prepare ourselves...but you can never really know what it will be like until it happens. Our family groups huddled around discussing the importance of telling the world how we're being treated...my husband and brothers warning me not to get involved – how could I not after Geert's death? The dignity of protest, the moral imperative of speaking out...

PRISONER 2
It's like the death of a loved one in here, you know how grief-stricken you're going to be; you try to prepare yourself by imagining the scene. But when it happens it's still utterly devastating. Of course we talked about it at home, how we'd cope, tricks to help us survive, analyzing their tactics in an attempt to give us some control. To keep the fear at bay...but I don't know why we fear death so much, we're already in hell.

(A moaning, sobbing noise is heard from the Isolation Cell SL.)

PRISONER 1
No, we're not in hell – she is. At least we've gone past the stage of utter fear. The confusion of those first days, the anxiety and terror at every sound, or imagined sound – not knowing where it was coming from. It was like being placed alive in a grave.

PRISONER 2
I know. At least we're in the main cell.

PRISONER 1
And it must be time for your dancing class.

PRISONER 2
Not today, I don't feel like it...

(PRISONER 1 drags PRISONER 2 reluctantly to her feet. They begin to dance the Cha Cha.)

PRISONER 1
Come on you know it's good for you. One two cha cha cha, three four cha cha cha. No, remember to ground the movement, don't bounce. This is meant to be sexy.

(The sound of the woman sobbing in the Isolation Cell continues again. PRISONER 2 stops dancing, but is forced to continue by PRISONER 1.)

PRISONER 1
No, come on. Sing as well…We'll help her when they bring her back. We can't do anything for her now.

(The two women continue to dance and hum 'La Cucaracha'. Lights fade on them.)

Scene Five

(Lights up on Captain's Office. He is on the telephone. The OFFICER continues to cut and paste in his scrapbook, he looks up at the CAPTAIN throughout the conversation.)

CAPTAIN
Yes sir. I have considered the material you sent…Yes I agree, a very generous budget. But of course we have our own methods here which can be just as effective and are much cheaper…No, of course…I agree completely…no, we cannot appear to be the poor relation…of course we must move with the times, show ourselves receptive to the new technological age. Ha, ha…yes those were my very words today to my Officer…But of course, a marvellous opportunity to 'do our bit' as you say sir…yes of course, forging important foreign links…Absolutely sir, exactly my sentiments. And it is for those very reasons, sir, that I am putting in an order for Stun belts from Sten Tech Inc…yes I know they come highly recommended and I thought some Black Rods…Well I thought one or two…cases?…Yes, yes two cases. Good that's finalised then…Of course not sir, pleased to be of assistance…
Oh there's no problem there sir, the doctor verified it, he's good isn't he?…oh something like 'eaten something incompatible with her health'…ha ha…ha ha, thank you sir I was quite pleased with it myself…One, in the Isolation Cell at the moment…a day or two I should think…early days at the moment sir, impossible to say…He starts tomorrow…yes isn't it? Just what we need to show him the ropes, break him in so to speak…Oh she's fine, thank you sir…yes and the grandchildren, can't imagine what I did without them. And your good lady?…Yes I'm sure she is. These things take a lot of organising…of course it must be right. It's her big day, and it'll give you just the right opportunity to polish up those medals sir…yes, yes an excellent achievement…My very best regards to all of you…Well what can I say? We'd be delighted to attend. Thank you so much. And also sir, thank you for keeping me in the picture. Yes goodbye…goodbye. *(Replaces receiver.)* Ha, ha. He's pleased.

OFFICER
And so are you by the looks of it. Got your wedding invitation then.

CAPTAIN
Yes, and I should bloody well think so. It'll be the event of the year…You're not still cutting and pasting are you?

OFFICER
You never know when this could be useful.

Scene Six

(Isolation Cell. PRISONER 3 in same position. She moves her head as if listening.)

PRISONER 3
Try to keep calm, nothing's happened yet. What to think about? My family…no, I can't. The main cell. They will return me, they can't keep me in here forever…? I can't breathe, or move or see. No I've never heard of them doing that. What have I heard of them doing?…We all know what they do…*(Begins to sob.)* I'm so…*(Long pause as she tries to contain her fear.)*.
The main cell. The main cell…with the other women to speak to…to be with. To touch. To *be* with…*be. (Pause as she rocks to comfort herself.)*. They will explain to me, I need to understand why I am here…Soon I'll be in there with them, in the main cell, the air will be so fresh. My mattress, warm. One day soon I will be free from this cell, I will be taken to the main cell with the other women. Then I will speak.

Scene Seven

(Captain's Office. CAPTAIN, OFFICER and New RECRUIT.)

CAPTAIN
Well, were your family pleased about your new position?

RECRUIT
Delighted sir.

CAPTAIN
And how do you feel on your first day?

RECRUIT
Very excited and eager to start learning sir.

CAPTAIN
Good. Keen to start learning eh? Well let's not make him wait any longer. *(To the OFFICER.)* Take the new boy with you when you go to the isolation cell. You know the procedure.

OFFICER
Should by now. Come on, follow me.

CAPTAIN
To begin with you will be spending most of the time watching and observing the Officer. Take advantage of his experience. Learn from him. Then when we think you are ready you can take a more active part.

(Lights fade on Captain's Office, up on Isolation Cell.
PRISONER 3 hears the two men coming, and tries to move away from them.)

OFFICER
So are you ready to speak to us yet? (Long pause.) Look puta, if you've nothing to hide, why do you refuse to speak? I would have thought we'd given you enough time to think about it? How much longer do you think we're prepared to wait?
(OFFICER bends down very close to the PRISONER'S face.)
Now come on, be a good girl. You don't want that pretty face ruined, do you? You know your husband won't be quite so fond of you when he sees his once pretty wife, scarred and deformed. *(He kisses her roughly and then pushes her away.)*
It really isn't worth it you know. We'll find out which of your family's involved, just as soon as they find out what's happening to you in here. You don't think any man worth the name would let his wife suffer for him do you? They'll be begging us to let them in when they know what we're doing to you in here. So why not save yourself the pain and humiliation and tell us before we have to force the issue?

(OFFICER waits, then stands up, looks at RECRUIT and shrugs. He then kicks the PRISONER between her legs. As she cries out and crumples forward, he follows the first kick with a second to the stomach. The RECRUIT winces and looks away. OFFICER leaves the cell and is followed by the RECRUIT. They return to the Captain's Office.)

CAPTAIN
Well?

OFFICER
Nothing.

CAPTAIN
No surprises there then. Stupid bitch. What does she think she's doing? And how about you *(To RECRUIT)*, what did you learn from your first lesson?
(RECRUIT looks at a loss to know what to say.)
Come on. You did go in with the Officer?

RECRUIT
Yes...sir.

CAPTAIN
And you watched him in action?

RECRUIT
Yes sir.

CAPTAIN
Well come on then, tell me what you learned from your first lesson?

RECRUIT
Well sir, I saw a woman in leg-irons and a blindfold refuse to give the Officer the information he wanted.

CAPTAIN
Good. Go on.

RECRUIT
I then saw the Officer kiss the woman and then kick her twice. Once in the...between her legs and the other in the stomach.

CAPTAIN
Hang on there, what did the Officer do before he kicked the woman? Are you telling me new boy that the Officer went straight into the cell, asked her a question, then started kicking her?

RECRUIT
Not exactly sir.

CAPTAIN
Well tell me exactly. I asked for an exact account of what happened in the cell. If you are going to learn you must watch, analyse and understand why. Now start again.

RECRUIT
I'm sorry sir. OK let me see. The Officer went into the cell and started speaking to the prisoner.

CAPTAIN
How? How did he speak to her? Was he shouting? Was he vicious? Was he reasonable? How did he speak to her?

RECRUIT
He didn't shout. But he was...wasn't...He started by asking her how much longer did he have to wait before she answered his questions. And the lady...

CAPTAIN
Prisoner 3.

RECRUIT
Sorry, Prisoner 3 refused to speak. He then tried to coax her into speaking by asking her to be a good girl and by telling her she was pretty and he didn't want to ruin her good looks. That's when her kissed her.

CAPTAIN
Why? Why do you think he kissed her?

RECRUIT
Um…I'm not really sure sir.

CAPTAIN
Guess, speculate…

RECRUIT
To um…because he wanted to let her know he could do anything he wanted?

CAPTAIN
That'll do to begin with. Carry on.

RECRUIT
Then she still wouldn't speak and he told her it was a waste of time because her family would give themselves up when they knew what was happening to her…here.

CAPTAIN
How did he explain all this?

RECRUIT
Quite gently sir.

CAPTAIN
Why do you think he didn't get angry?

RECRUIT
Because that would have made her more frightened?

CAPTAIN
At this stage how would you assess the Officer's behaviour?

RECRUIT
I think he was quite patient with the prisoner, and he was trying to coax her into speaking.

CAPTAIN
And the prisoner?

RECRUIT
She was very frightened...

CAPTAIN
Do you think it was reasonable of her not to speak after the Officer had asked her in a kindly and patient way?

RECRUIT
No sir. She seemed determined not to give in.

CAPTAIN
Stubborn?

RECRUIT
Yes, stubborn.

CAPTAIN
You know they say stubbornness is the last refuge of the weak? OK carry on.

RECRUIT
Well when it was obvious she wasn't going to speak the Officer kicked her twice. Once between the legs and the other in the stomach.

CAPTAIN
How did you feel when you saw that?

RECRUIT
Shocked...and...horrified sir.

CAPTAIN
Shocked and horrified? Why?

RECRUIT
Because I was brought up to believe that men should never hit women...sir.

OFFICER
OK...So what did you do?

RECRUIT
Do?

CAPTAIN
Yes do. What did you do? As you were so shocked and horrified, surely you did something? Tried to prevent the Officer?

RECRUIT
I didn't do anything sir.

CAPTAIN
Didn't do anything? Why?

RECRUIT
Because the Officer is my superior sir and I didn't know what to do.

CAPTAIN
Do you think I have faith in my Officer?

RECRUIT
Yes sir.

CAPTAIN
Why would I put my trust in my Officer, new boy?

RECRUIT
Because he does his work well and is a good Officer.

CAPTAIN
Good. Yes he is a good Officer, who knows exactly what he's doing and why.
Now, why do you think he kicked the prisoner?

RECRUIT
Because she annoyed him because she wouldn't speak.

CAPTAIN
Did he seem annoyed? Did he lose his temper or appear to be angry?

RECRUIT
No sir, he was very calm.

CAPTAIN
Well that can't be the reason can it? Try again.

RECRUIT
Well…because…he wanted to warn her that he wasn't going to put up with her
stubbornness anymore.

CAPTAIN
And?...

RECRUIT
That he'd given her enough chances.

CAPTAIN
Any more?

RECRUIT
And he was showing her that he was in charge and not her.

CAPTAIN
Mmm. Quite reasonable behaviour in the circumstances then? You realise that she comes from a family of dissidents don't you? They are at this moment working to undermine the government? And that she is protecting them because they think we will take pity on a woman? You see now why he had to try to get the information from her? And he didn't touch her pretty little face did he?

RECRUIT
No sir, I understand more fully now sir that he behaved with patience and restraint.

CAPTAIN
I will repeat my original question new boy. What have you learned from your first lesson?

RECRUIT
That when dealing with people...

CAPTAIN
Dissidents...

RECRUIT
Dissidents, first try to coax them into speaking. Try not to make them too afraid. Be patient and restrained.

CAPTAIN
And?

RECRUIT
But then...if they refuse to comply we have to show them who is in charge, for the sake of the stability of the country.

CAPTAIN
Well done. A good first lesson. Now as a reward I want you to go back to the isolation cell and release the prisoner from her leg-irons, untie her hands and remove the blindfold. Then return her to the Main Cell. *(He hands the RECRUIT a key.)* Be vigilant. Take account of how she reacts and also the behaviour of the other two women in the Main Cell. This is how you will learn.

RECRUIT
Thank you sir.

(RECRUIT leaves the Captain's Office, but it remains lit. He goes to the Isolation Cell and tentatively enters. The PRISONER is clearly frightened. The

RECRUIT unties her blindfold, and smiles at her reassuringly. She returns his smile. He then carefully unties her hands and unlocks the leg-irons. He gently helps her to her feet and leads her to the Main Cell. He opens the door and takes her in. PRISONER 1 crosses to her and takes her hands. She leads her to a mattress where she is joined by PRISONER 2. They both begin to rub her hands and legs where she has been bound. The RECRUIT watches from the entrance to the cell.)

PRISONER 3
(Looking up at the RECRUIT.) Thank you...for bringing me to the main cell.

(RECRUIT smiles and exits. He returns to the Captain's Office. Main Cell remains lit.)

CAPTAIN
Well?

RECRUIT
Prisoner safely returned to the Main Cell sir.

CAPTAIN
And how was she?

RECRUIT
She seemed very grateful sir and pleased to be with the others.

CAPTAIN
Did she appear stubborn or obstinate?

RECRUIT
Not at all sir she was very...pleasant.

CAPTAIN
Pleasant eh? Then it would seem as if our good Officer here has done the trick. Do you think so?

RECRUIT
Well from my observations and analysis sir, I would suggest she might be more willing to tell us about her family now than she was before. She seemed grateful to me sir for releasing her.

CAPTAIN
How did that feel?

RECRUIT
I was pleased to be helping sir.

CAPTAIN
Let's leave them alone for a while to relish their companionship. We'll try again with her later. In the meantime new boy, let me give you your second lesson for today – how I like my coffee served.

(CAPTAIN and OFFICER laugh together. RECRUIT smiles and then joins in with the other two. Lights dim on Captain's Office.)

Scene Eight

PRISONER 1
What did they do?

PRISONER 3
Nothing…much. Do you know why I'm here?

PRISONER 1
Who knows for certain with this lot? It could be anything or nothing. But probably it's linked to the people you know, or your family.

PRISONER 2
It's a Government strategy of targeting women. They arrest the women in the hope that their degradation will break the spirit of male militants.

PRISONER 1
They know, you see, that the humiliation of a wife, mother or sister will break a man's back.

PRISONER 3
Then they don't really want information?

PRISONER 1
I doubt it. They probably know whatever there is to know about you, or you wouldn't be here. After they've had their fun they'll probably return you to your family. That way they'll appear just. But you'll also serve as a constant reminder to the community of their overall power. It creates an atmosphere of fear.

PRISONER 3
They want us to leave our village to make way for some new scheme they have for the area. Some of them refuse…But not me, I haven't done anything…You think they want my husband…or father?

PRISONER 2
Are they involved?

PRISONER 3
My mother's terrified. We've heard what they're doing in other villages.

PRISONER 1
My village was one.

PRISONER 3
Is that why you're here?

PRISONER 1
Could be. I spoke out…

PRISONER 2
It's probably more to do with us going on strike. The company must have
passed our names onto the Government.

PRISONER 3
But strikes are legal.

PRISONER 1
Since when has being legal meant anything…Is it legal to destroy whole
villages, to play football with the heads of young men?…How can we sit by
and do nothing?…

PRISONER 2
Strikes are legal for the benefit of the outside world and foreign trade. But just
try putting it into action. Look, the oil companies, and many others as well,
don't want strikes hitting their profits and the Government sees all strikers as
subversives, enemies of the state. One tells the other and they instruct this lot to
do their dirty work.

PRISONER 1
Here have some of this. We saved it for you. *(Gives PRISONER 3 some food
saved from their own rations.)* It's not that bad. We think there must be a visit
due.

PRISONER 3
Visit?

PRISONER 2
The eternal optimist here is convinced that because the food's improved, we're
going to get some kind of official visit. From abroad, or something.

PRISONER 3
Then things could improve? We could be released?

PRISONER 2
Don't build you hopes up; she's always like this.

PRISONER 1
It's as good an indication as any. We can't be taken unawares.

PRISONER 3
But what can we do?

PRISONER 2
Nothing.

PRISONER 1
Rubbish. Did you see the new recruit? They haven't got to him yet. What say we risk asking him for books and paper, pens, you know. Tell him we need something to stop us from going mad with boredom?

PRISONER 2
What?

PRISONER 1
He might be more sympathetic...

PRISONER 3
He certainly seems better than the others.

PRISONER 1
It's worth a try...

PRISONER 2
Not a hope.

PRISONER 1
Whose side are you on?

PRISONER 3
But what'll we do if we get it?

PRISONER 2
Good question.

PRISONER 1
Perhaps we could smuggle a letter out. Try to explain what's happening. If only people knew what was going on. There they are lying on the beaches, swimming in the sea, getting to know the locals. What do they think is going on behind these walls? If they knew that as they were rubbing on the sun oil people were being rubbed with acid; as they were learning the local songs,

locals were having their tongues ripped out; as they were swilling the cheap and fruity wines we were being forced to drink paint stripper; as their feet move to the newly learned dances ours are being beaten till they bleed. That as their planes disappear from view taking them back to the security of their homes, we have to learn another meaning for 'disappear'. If they knew, they would do something. How could they not? We must tell them. I'll ask the new recruit for paper and pencils.

PRISONER 2
I don't understand where you continue to get it from.

PRISONER 1
What?

PRISONER 2
Hope. Surely after all you've seen and experienced you realize that people do know and are not doing anything. That most people aren't interested if it doesn't involve them. That they will find all sorts of reasons for ignoring or even justifying atrocities. That most people really don't care. Oh they might mutter and tut, but when it comes down to actually doing anything, they're not interested. I mean, we're not expecting people not to go on holiday, we're just asking them not to come here. But they can't even do that. *(Begins to mock comments made by the tourists.)* "It's such a lovely place, really unspoilt. And so cheap! Do you know we had a local meal for next to nothing?…wine as well. Where else could you get such value for money?"

(PRISONER 1 joins in.)

PRISONER 1
"And the people are so nice. We felt really safe. No crime on the streets, so different from home. We could learn a thing or two from them. They respect their police."

PRISONER 2
"And the way they work, never stop, nothing too much trouble for them."

PRISONER 1
"I didn't see anything wrong there…"

PRISONER 2
"No, nor me. No sign of anything wrong at all…and anyway…"

PRISONER 1
"…You'd never go anywhere if you believed all you read, would you?"

PRISONER 2
"And what could we do about it? But you know, they probably behave better

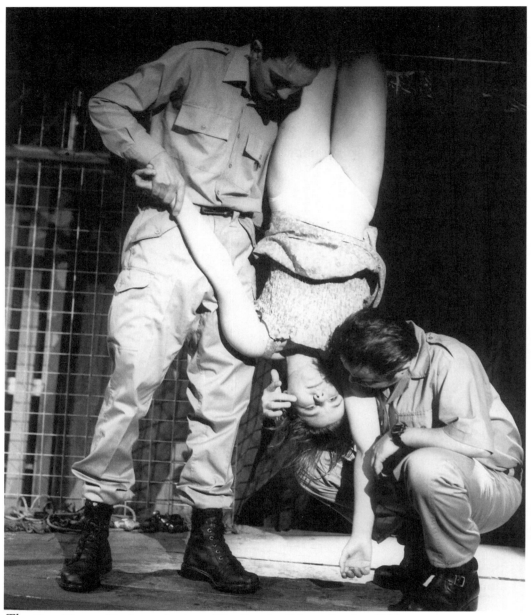

The New Theatre Works production of Shading the Crime, *October 1998.*
Directed by Ellie Parker at the Courtyard Theatre, Hereford.

because we are here – we're probably helping by being here…an' if not…"

PRISONER 1
"Not our business is it? We work hard for our holiday, we deserve it…"

PRISONER 2
"Smashing holiday…"

PRISONER 1
"Smashing"…Yes, you're right; I know you're right. But I still have hope, I have to have. When I think about what has happened to me and my family, my son…I think human beings are the cruellest, most despicable creatures in existence. Then I think about what I've become through all that. How from nearly being destroyed I survived, to become strong and more resilient. That despite all the suffering and fear that surrounds us, I have become calmer and more rational. I can continue living and fighting because of this intangible thing called hope. I can't let them take that away. Otherwise I'm finished, defeated.

PRISONER 2
Well if you're willing to risk it, we could give it a try.

PRISONER 1
Yes we will. Good that's the plan sorted out, now time for fun.

PRISONER 3
Fun?

PRISONER 2
Oh no, not again. I thought you'd forgotten today.

PRISONER 1
As if I'd forget the dance lesson.

PRISONER 3
What?

PRISONER 1
No not you, not today anyway – you need to rest. Up you get. *(Pulls PRISONER 2 to her feet.)*

PRISONER 2
It's her idea of positive action to keep our spirits up.

PRISONER 1
Do you always end up enjoying it?

PRISONER 2
Yes, I suppose so.

PRISONER 1
Then for once admit it. You do enjoy it.

(The two women begin the cha cha, humming to 'La Cucaracha'. PRISONER 3 enjoys watching them.)

PRISONER 2
What will we do when I've learned this one?

PRISONER 1
I don't know. I've taught you all I know. We'll have to go over them all again I suppose. Perfect them.

PRISONER 3
I know lots of dances – foreign and traditional. My mother is a wonderful dancer, she taught us all to dance. And to sing. I know many songs. Perhaps I could teach you some, if you would like me to?

PRISONER 2
I think that would be excellent. Anything for a break from this. *(She tries to sit down.)*

PRISONER 1
Oh no you don't. This is good for you. We'll sing after.

(They continue to dance. The overall mood is much lighter.)

Scene Nine

(Captain's Office.)

CAPTAIN
Who the hell do they think they are, asking for paper and pens? And what kind of a fool are you for listening and running their errands?

RECRUIT
I'm sorry sir I just thought that…

CAPTAIN
Listen, go back and tell them, especially No.1 – she's probably behind this – that, no, we will not give them book, pens, papers or anything. Why should I care if they are bored? What do they expect…degree courses in psychology…weekly cabarets…?

OFFICER
Ye' contortion and disappearing acts a speciality…

(RECRUIT goes to leave but is called back by the CAPTAIN.)

CAPTAIN
No, no hang on. Maybe that's not the best way given the circumstances. Can you suggest anything?

OFFICER
How about some sewing, women are meant to be good at sewing. Could prove useful too. Why make our women work when we can let them do it?

CAPTAIN
Excellent. Two birds with one stone. Good constructive work. No one could possibly complain – safe as well. Who cares if they try to smuggle darned socks out of the country? Ha ha. A great idea. Go and tell them the good news boy, but in future be more alert.

(RECRUIT leaves the office. He makes his way along to the Main Cell. Both areas are lit. As he reaches the Main Cell he can hear the women talking inside. He listens.)

PRISONER 1
Well...there was a lot of fighting and smoke. We were running to hide behind a bush away from the soldiers. I ran ahead with the baby, my son was right behind me...until they grabbed him. I fell. I heard the soldier say, "Kill them all", then another said, "Don't be stupid we have to take the boy".

PRISONER 3
Then what happened?

PRISONER 2
That was the last she saw of him. We've asked after him, everywhere...but they told us he'd been taken to an orphanage because he was 'morally and materially abandoned'. He'd been adopted. They said they couldn't trace him. We've tried everything, we've even spoken to foreign journalists, but no one seems able to help.

PRISONER 3
Are you sure he's alive?

PRISONER 1
No...it could all be lies. They could have killed him when they took him because he was a boy, but I have to carry on looking until I know, without question.

PRISONER 3
But after all this time surely...

PRISONER 1
He's still *my* son, no matter where he is or what he's been told...

PRISONER 3
Do these police know all this?

PRISONER 2
Of course, they know everything…they're all in on it…

PRISONER 3
But what about the journalists…didn't they report it?

PRISONER 2
Oh yes, they kept their promise, but the ambassador just denied it, like he denies any of this is happening.

PRISONER 1
But that's no reason to stop; we have this visit to plan for…

PRISONER 3
I'm not sure…I just want to be released…to be back with my family.

PRISONER 1
You can't think like that. You owe it to your family to try whatever you can.

PRISONER 2
You don't really think it's going to end with your release do you? You and your family and friends are, for whatever reason, marked. You have their attention and they don't let go easily.

PRISONER 1
Once we give in we're all finished. They'll feel free to destroy any village, or any worker who gets in their way. It's the only way we have to face the future.

(RECRUIT enters the cell.)

RECRUIT
Your request for pens and paper has been denied. But the Captain has decided to be lenient and to give you some sewing to alleviate your boredom.

PRISONER 1
But we don't want to sew. Do you think women are only good for sewing?

RECRUIT
The decision has nothing to do with me. Your request has already got me in trouble with the Captain. Be grateful you're getting anything.

PRISONER 1
Look we're sorry if we got you into trouble. We just think you seem kind.

PRISONER 2
Too kind to be working here. We have to stay but you don't. You can go. Go on; get out before it's too late for you.

PRISONER 1
You can make more of a difference by helping us than by working with those monsters. Don't waste your life like this...you're just a boy...

RECRUIT
I returned Prisoner 3 because I was ordered to. You think that because I'm new you can treat me like a fool? You are trying to use me. To set me against my superiors. Well those are the people from whom I take my orders and don't you forget it. I was employed for this job because I have qualities like them. You will be given sewing – like it or not.

(RECRUIT leaves the Main Cell and returns to the Captain's Office.)

CAPTAIN
Well what did they say?

RECRUIT
They didn't want the sewing, but I told them they had no choice and that they should be grateful to you sir.

CAPTAIN
Good...didn't let them sweet talk you this time then boy?

RECRUIT
Of course not sir. I won't let that happen again. In fact sir, before I was entering the cell I heard the women talking, so I stood outside and listened.

OFFICER
Well what a turn up. We've recruited quite a little snake in the grass, Captain...eh?

CAPTAIN
Yes, he's beginning to shape up nicely. Now tell us, Special Policeman 467, what did you hear?

RECRUIT
I heard Prisoner 1 telling Prisoner 3 about how a young boy...

CAPTAIN
Her son.

RECRUIT
Yes sir her son, how he was taken by soldiers.

CAPTAIN
Did you hear when?

RECRUIT
No sir, but I sensed it must have been some time ago because she has been looking for him ever since it happened.

CAPTAIN
And what has she been told?

RECRUIT
That he'd been put in an orphanage because he was 'morally and materially abandoned'.

CAPTAIN
Yes. It happened frequently during the uprising. But you're too young to remember that.

(OFFICER gets scrapbook and shows the RECRUIT.)

OFFICER
These dissidents abandoned their own children, and we made sure they were looked after. That they would grow to love their country and serve their government. But do we get thanks for that? No, the mothers are now so ashamed of their actions that they make up sob stories for the world to hear. But you're not fooled, are you boy?

RECRUIT
No of course not sir. In fact I have heard of these stories from my father.

CAPTAIN
You see now why she's still causing trouble, she is racked with guilt. But it's easier for her to blame us than admit to the truth.

OFFICER
What kind of women would abandon their own children? Can you imagine your mother behaving in such a way?

RECRUIT
Of course not sir, never.

OFFICER
And what if you'd found out that she had?

RECRUIT
I would disown her sir. It is appalling to think of it.

CAPTAIN
Of course it is and you're lucky that you come from such a good family. But you see what we're up against here don't you? We have to be ever vigilant that these aberrations of nature are not allowed to undermine our country.

RECRUIT
I also heard them planning to cause trouble during a visit they think is going to take place…

CAPTAIN
Really?

RECRUIT
That's why they wanted the paper and pens sir.

OFFICER
That's why they're getting sewing.

RECRUIT
Yes, ha ha, yes sir. That's very clever.

CAPTAIN
We think so, but if they suspect there is a visit they will be looking for every excuse to slander us. We must make sure they get no opportunity to complain. We must make them comfortable, eh? *(Nods across to the OFFICER.)*

OFFICER
Here take them their sewing. But take them these as well. *(Hands the RECRUIT a packet of sanitary towels.)* Well don't look so shocked; you know what they are don't you?

RECRUIT
Of course sir, but I've never had anything to do with this sort of thing before.

OFFICER
Oh for god's sake boy, grow up! All you have to do is to take them to the cell and ask if anyone needs them. You don't have to put the bloody thing on. You didn't think that's what we wanted, did you? *(Laughing.)*

CAPTAIN
What do you take us for Special Policeman? Now go on. You're doing very well you know.

RECRUIT
Thank you sir. *(Laughs in an embarrassed way.)* Thank you, I'll just take these things through then, shall I?

OFFICER
467…keep on the alert. We expect you to report back on exactly what happens when you give them the sewing…and the towels. OK?

RECRUIT
Of course sir. I won't be caught out by them again.

(RECRUIT exits. CAPTAIN and OFFICER smile at each other.)

CAPTAIN
He's responding well. I think we can risk moving on to the next stage.

OFFICER
Mmm…very keen. I thought he would be, but you can never tell for sure.

(Lights fade to blackout on whole stage.)

Scene Ten

(Lights up on Isolation Cell. The OFFICER and RECRUIT have PRISONER 3 between them. She is struggling and screaming in panic. The RECRUIT looks uneasy.)

OFFICER
Come on, I need your help. Keep hold of her.

RECRUIT
I'm trying but she…

(Officer punches her in the stomach and she goes limp.)

OFFICER
That's better. Now help me with her legs.

RECRUIT
What are we doing?

OFFICER
Put her legs in the straps. Go on before she starts struggling again.

RECRUIT
But she's the one who's bleeding…

OFFICER
I know, idiot. You told us remember?

RECRUIT
But what's the point?

OFFICER
Ever heard of septicaemia…blood poisoning? Most effective…leaves no marks either. Now get on with it.

(RECRUIT fastens PRISONER 3's ankles in the straps, whilst the OFFICER stands over him. The OFFICER indicates to the RECRUIT to lift the pole. They both lift the pole and place the ends in two fixtures on the wall. PRISONER 3 hangs upside down. Her skirt falls about her face revealing her legs. The RECRUIT moves to pull the skirt back up, but the OFFICER indicates to the cell door. They leave the cell and exit. Lights dim on the Isolation Cell but the PRISONER remains visible. Lights up on Main Cell.)

PRISONER 2
Stupid little fool, why did she take them? She fell right into their trap.

PRISONER 1
We should have warned her. I wonder how long they'll keep her?

(Long pause. PRISONER 2 screams at the cell door.)

PRISONER 2
BASTARDS!…BASTARDS!

PRISONER 1
Jesus…they really don't care do they? Even with the visit…

PRISONER 2
Oh shut up…shut up…shut up! There's obviously not going to be a visit! *(Pause)*. How can you believe there's still going to be a visit after this? If we hadn't pushed the new one, they may have left us alone for a while.

PRISONER 1
That's rubbish and you know it. You think we're dealing with rational people here?

PRISONER 2
Yes, yes I do. I think they are so rational it's frightening. They know exactly what they're doing. They know exactly how to play the new recruit, they know how to trap us, they know how to hurt us. Nothing is left to chance, can't you see?

PRISONER 1
Yes I can, I can see. You're right. Why would they give us this sewing? Everything they do is for a purpose.

PRISONER 2
Oh I get it…we're going to have a visit and so they give us some sewing to do?

PRISONER 1
Yes. That's exactly what they do. They use torture which leaves no physical marks, but will terrorize us into behaving ourselves. They give us sewing because it will look as if they're being considerate, but which they think is harmless.

PRISONER 2
Think is harmless? It's useless. What can we do with a needle and thread, sew a distress signal?

PRISONER 1
If that's all there is, yes that's what we'll have to do…

(PRISONER 2 groans then resumes her yelling.)

PRISONER 2
BASTARDS!…

(Lights fade on the Main Cell, but the two women remain visible. PRISONER 2 eventually slumps onto the mattress whilst PRISONER 1 paces around the cell.)

(Lights up on Captain's Office.)

CAPTAIN
I think you're worrying unnecessarily. You forget how easy it is.

OFFICER
Well I don't want some snot-nosed kid fucking things up that's all. I know who'd get the blame…well I recommended him didn't I?

CAPTAIN
We've still got plenty of time. Don't worry. Look you're forgetting the three golden rules. All we need to create the perfect interrogator is…?

OFFICER
Carefully staged training – unquestioning obedience.

CAPTAIN
Induction…go on…

OFFICER
Financial advantages and status.

The New Theatre Works production of Shading the Crime, *October 1998.*
Directed by Ellie Parker at the Courtyard Theatre, Hereford.

CAPTAIN
It worked for you. It will for him. It's all going to plan.

(RECRUIT enters the office.)

CAPTAIN
Come in Special Policeman 467. We're very pleased with your progress. You know why you were chosen to help the Officer with Prisoner 3, don't you?

RECRUIT
No sir.

CAPTAIN
Because you've proven we can trust you. Your information about Prisoner 3 was vital.

RECRUIT
But I didn't realise what you were going to do sir.

CAPTAIN
You wouldn't have told us if you'd known? Is that what you're saying? That you would defend the very people who are trying to undermine your country? The country which has supported you and your family, the country which is making sure you are professionally trained for a job so that in time you too may have a family. You place mothers who abandon their children, who blow up innocent victims, whose behaviour is less than human above decent people like your own family? Is that what you're saying?

RECRUIT
No of course not sir. And I appreciate the chance you're giving me to be someone.

OFFICER
So what are you concerned about then 467?

RECRUIT
Nothing sir, it's just I'm …unaccustomed with…

OFFICER
With what?

RECRUIT
With what you asked me to do.

CAPTAIN
'Playing on the swings'?

RECRUIT
What?

CAPTAIN
That's what we call that particular activity…you might find it easier to say. Go on try it. Tell me what you did today.

RECRUIT
Today I helped a prisoner 'play on the swings'.

CAPTAIN
Easier?

RECRUIT
Yes sir…yes it is.

CAPTAIN
So I wonder how our friend is getting on 'playing on the swings'. Ha ha. I think one of us should go and check, don't you Officer?

OFFICER
Yes sir…and I think we owe it to 467 to let him check it out. After all, as you observed, he caught her out.

CAPTAIN
Whatever you say…whatever you say.

OFFICER
OK, Special Policemen 467, go into the Isolation Cell and guard the prisoner. Don't talk to her, just make sure you tell us if she passes out for a significant length of time…more than three days and that could be a problem…It's OK son, I'm only joking. That's not the result we're after with this one. An' don't worry about the noises she makes, they'll try anything on to get sympathy. Orders understood?

RECRUIT
Yes sir.

OFFICER
Well go on then. Who knows you may be helping us with a 'tea party' soon.

CAPTAIN
A 'tea party with toast' even.

OFFICER
We might even let you be mother.

(Lights fade on Captain's Office. Lights up on Isolation Cell.)

(RECRUIT leaves the Captain's Office and goes into the Isolation Cell. The PRISONER is groaning and sobbing. The RECRUIT stands to the side of her facing out to the audience. He closes his eyes, but stands motionless.)

Scene Eleven

(Lights up on Captain's Office. CAPTAIN is sifting through promotional brochures. He hands some to the OFFICER who is sitting in the other chair.)

OFFICER
Do you think it'll happen?

CAPTAIN
Almost there.

OFFICER
But Interpol holding a National Conference here? I can't see it.

CAPTAIN
I tell you this is just the beginning. Next the Tourist Centre of the Year, followed by foreign investment.

OFFICER
What about the human rights angle?

CAPTAIN
We'll deny it. Where money's involved people are only too eager to believe what they want. And anyway where's the proof? I think the boy's had long enough, go and get him. Let him help you get the prisoner down.

OFFICER
And return her to the Main Cell?

CAPTAIN
Yeah, but watch his reactions.

(OFFICER leaves Office and goes to the Isolation Cell. The RECRUIT opens his eyes and his face takes on a blank expression. Together they untie the Prisoner. They take her to the Main Cell. The RECRUIT opens the door and roughly pushes her in. The other two women place her on the mattress.)

OFFICER
Captain wants a word with you.

RECRUIT
Have I done anything wrong sir?

OFFICER
On the contrary, he's very pleased.

(They enter the office. Lights dim on the Office, and up on the Main Cell. The Isolation Cell is still dimly visible.)

Scene Twelve

PRISONER 1
There is something we can do.

PRISONER 2
What?

PRISONER 1
We can use the needles and the thread to protest.

PRISONER 2
What are you talking about? How can we? You're being ridiculous. Admit it we're beaten.

PRISONER 1
No we're not. We have to be as cunning as they are. We'll play them just like they play us.

PRISONER 2
Go on...

PRISONER 1
If we try not to antagonise them, and dutifully do any sewing they give us, they may just think we've been warned off.

PRISONER 2
But then if there is a visit, we play into their hands. We won't be able to speak to them, we'll be here sewing. No one will know what we're all suffering. What a waste after everything that's happened.

PRISONER 1
No it won't all be wasted. Think about what you've said. We won't be able to speak to them. The likelihood is we'll be shown to them, why else would they give us extra food. They'll probably smarten up the cell, show whoever it is around, but they'd never leave us alone with them, to speak to them would they? So we make our silence alarming, striking. Something no one will be able

to ignore.

PRISONER 2
How?

PRISONER 1
We'll sew our lips together.

PRISONER 2
What!?

PRISONER 1
Sew our lips together. Think of the visual impact. Why else would we do such an extreme act unless we were compelled to by extreme circumstances? We wouldn't need to speak it would be clear for all to see.

PRISONER 2
Jesus…but would we do it ourselves or to each other?

PRISONER 1
I don't know…

PRISONER 2
And how would we know when to do it?

PRISONER 1
I don't know…I don't know.

(Lights dim.)

Act Two

Scene One

(RECRUIT takes PRISONER 1 from the Main Cell into the Captain's Office. There have been significant changes made to the Main Cell. It has been smartened up and is more comfortable.)

CAPTAIN
Sit down. I want to talk to you. Now I'm not a stupid man, and hope for your sake you're not a stupid woman. I know for instance that you are the driving force in the Main Cell. The other two depend on you, and will follow your lead. Well I have a proposition to put to you. As you know, we have for some years now been trying to gain international recognition, to develop our reputation worldwide both as a holiday destination, and also in terms of foreign trade and

commerce. Well we now have the chance. People are interested in us. We are going to receive a visit from influential foreign visitors. Their approbation is all we need for the rest of the world to follow. You don't look shocked.

PRISONER 1
The extra food and the new facilities...

CAPTAIN
Ha ha, yes I thought you would suspect. Well I can assure you that no one is going to threaten our chances, no one is going to stand in the way of this country's progress and acceptance. Which of course brings me to you. I want you to sign this confession. I want you to admit to these crimes and to sign this declaration which states that you have been treated fairly and with compassion. If you do not do so immediately, you will do so eventually. Once you sign so will the others.

(Long pause.)

PRISONER 1
What will happen if I sign it?

CAPTAIN
We will keep you here until after the visit and then release you.

PRISONER 1
How can I trust you?

CAPTAIN
How can you not?

PRISONER 1
Can we meet the visitors?

CAPTAIN
No. No one is allowed to speak to them.

PRISONER 1
Will we see them? Will you bring them to the cell, to show them how healthy we are. How well we are treated with our new furniture and our sewing?

CAPTAIN
Of course, but no one will be allowed to speak to them. That is a stipulation.

PRISONER 1
What if they ask to speak to us? What if they insist on it?

CAPTAIN
How touchingly naive you are. You don't think they are actually coming here to discover anything do you? No...oh no. This is one gigantic PR job. They want to trade with us, we with them. It would be bad for business if these filthy lies about human rights were not investigated and refuted once and for all. That is why they are coming. No one really cares, not once it starts to cut into their profits.

PRISONER 1
There are some people out there who care you know.

CAPTAIN
Not the ones with power. No one's even heard of you. Come on sign. We don't want any mess do we?

PRISONER 1
If I sign, how can I be sure we will see the visitors?

CAPTAIN
They have to see you. It's part of the agreement. Now for your own sake, sign.

PRISONER 1
If I confess to guilt then I betray my family and friends...I'll be putting them at risk.

CAPTAIN
You will regret it if you don't.

PRISONER 1
No. I will not do it. All I will promise is that I will not speak to the visitors. I will not condemn myself, my family or my friends with lies.

CAPTAIN
Foolish decision and one I can guarantee you will regret. *(to the RECRUIT)* Go and find the Officer. I need his help. Then wait for us in the Isolation Cell.
(RECRUIT leaves Office.)
He's coming along well. Well brought up, to be respectful of his family and superiors. How old would you say he was? Go on guess.
(OFFICER enters.)
Ah good he's found you. I was just telling Prisoner 1 that our new recruit is doing well. But he was carefully selected by my Officer here. Tell her how you know him.

OFFICER
I've kept my eye on him since we took him to the orphanage.

CAPTAIN
Tell her more…yes go on.

OFFICER
Well during one of the raids we were chasing some suspected dissidents. We'd been ordered to capture the children so they could be adopted by suitable families. Turn out to be useful to the government. We were chasing a woman and her two children. One was a boy of about three, the other was a baby. As the mother was running in front the poor little lad fell behind so we picked him up to take him to people who knew how to look after him. Lucky I was there. My mate thought they should all be shot orders or not, but he had no brain. We got quite a bit for every kid we handed in.

PRISONER 1
You're lying. I don't believe you. It's the oldest trick in the book. I know you know my history, I know how you think.

CAPTAIN
Carry on Officer.

(OFFICER gets scrapbook and gives it to PRISONER 1.)

OFFICER
Well I thought it might be useful to know what happened to them, so I kept track of as many as I could. This one went to a respectable, hard working family. Staunch supporters of the government, and times are hard for everyone, so when I knew he was looking for work I suggested he might be the right sort of material for our particular profession.

CAPTAIN
Seems he was right. The boy's shaping up nicely. And the family are very proud of their son. Grateful too. Well as his status has risen, so has theirs. How old would he be now? Seventeen if I'm not mistaken.

PRISONER 1
You've no proof. And don't think I'd believe him any more than you.

CAPTAIN
Who would you believe? Your own son? His adopted parents? We can easily arrange it. But why bother with all the pain of the past? Just sign the confession and make it easy for yourself. *(Pause, takes scrapbook from her.)*…What do you think is the worst thing that could happen to a mother? To lose her child? You think the worst thing has already happened to you? No I don't think so. I think the worst is yet to come. You have one last chance. Will you sign?

PRISONER 1
No.

CAPTAIN
You are a very stupid woman. For you will never be sure that what I say is a lie. I can guarantee you will live to regret this decision.

PRISONER 1
No more than if I betrayed my family, friends...

CAPTAIN
Oh I think so...yes, I think so for sure. I intend to make it so. Take her to the Isolation Cell, the boy's waiting...We'll find out now just how successful we've been with his induction.

Scene Two

(OFFICER takes PRISONER 1 to the Isolation Cell. The RECRUIT is waiting for them. The OFFICER pushes the woman to her knees.)

OFFICER
Tie her up, but don't blindfold her. Watch her.

(OFFICER leaves. The RECRUIT does as he is told. PRISONER 1 stares at him.)

RECRUIT
It's no good trying anything on me, I know my job. You can stare all you want. I know about people like you.

PRISONER 1
You should, you're one of us...really.

RECRUIT
Hmm...joking aren't you? I wouldn't be seen dead doing what you do.

PRISONER 1
But you can live with what you do?
(Pause. RECRUIT doesn't answer.)
Why don't you get out, before it's too late?...You're not responsible for what's happened...yet. You will be soon. Then you'll never break free...Get out while you still can.

RECRUIT
You're the one tied up. You're the one responsible for killing people. How dare you tell me I'm not free...lecture me on how to behave? I do what I want, nobody makes me.

PRISONER 1
They've done a good job on you...how old are you?...Do your family know what you're being trained to do...I mean actually trained to do?...What have you told them so far? What do you say when they ask each evening when you return home?
(Pause. RECRUIT begins to look uncomfortable.)
You haven't been home have you? Of course, they'll keep you here until the job's completed. Well you are in with a chance then. Get out, get away before it's too late.

RECRUIT
If you know what's good for you you'll just shut up. Sign or confess or whatever they ask. But don't waste your time giving me advice. A position with the special police unit is not to be turned down. I inspire respect. I am helping to maintain a country I was brought up in, and which I am proud of...it's a good job.

PRISONER 1
They?

RECRUIT
What?

PRISONER 1
They, you said. 'Do whatever they ask'. Not we.

(OFFICER enters with CAPTAIN.)

OFFICER
Talkative, is she? What's she been saying? Told you about the bombs she's planted, the innocent people she's killed? Told you about her son has she? Do you know Special Policeman 467 that this great freedom fighter was so determined to save her own skin that she abandoned her own three-year-old child? But of course you know that, you told us didn't you? Can you imagine your own mother doing that? Can you?

RECRUIT
No Sir. She never would do such a thing. No matter what.

OFFICER
What do you think of women like this Special Policeman?

RECRUIT
They're...inhuman Sir. They don't deserve to have children.

CAPTAIN
No they certainly don't. How old are you 467? Seventeen isn't it?

RECRUIT
Yes Sir.

CAPTAIN
Do you realise that her son was abandoned fourteen years ago? And that if he's still alive today, he'd be your age? In fact you could be her son.

RECRUIT
I could in years Sir, but I have a mother and father. I have a family who love me and have cared for me.

CAPTAIN
Ah yes of course, but who amongst us can be one hundred per cent sure of our bloodlines? Can you imagine finding out that this cunt kneeling at your feet was in fact your own mother? The woman who has murdered without remorse, plotted against the security of the state and even worse abandoned her own little baby?

PRISONER 1
You filthy torturing liars…*(OFFICER slaps her in the face with the back of his hand.)*

CAPTAIN
Thank you Officer. As I was saying Special Policeman 467, how would you feel to have this whore's blood in your veins?

RECRUIT
It's too disgusting to think about…I haven't got it in my veins Sir. She's not my mother. My mother would never abandon me…never.

CAPTAIN
And if you found out that she had…would you care what happened to her?

RECRUIT
No Captain…not at all. If she had abandoned me, I could not think of her as my mother.

CAPTAIN
Would you care what you did to her?

RECRUIT
No Sir…no, she would deserve anything that came to her…

PRISONER 1
You fool, you bloody fool. They're playing you like a fiddle. Can't you see what the murderers are doing? They're the murderers, not me!

(OFFICER moves to hit the prisoner but is stopped by the CAPTAIN.)

CAPTAIN
No...not you this time. After all it's the special policeman she's called a fool. Are you going to stand there and let this piece of filth, who is no better than the shit on the sole of your shoe abuse you? Go on...but mind the face. Go on...unless of course you think she is your mother?

(RECRUIT moves towards her and kicks her in the stomach. He looks back at the CAPTAIN who smiles and indicates to do it again. He does.)

OFFICER
A lot of filth came out of her mouth, I think she needs it washing out.

CAPTAIN
What do you think Special Policeman 467?

RECRUIT
Yes Sir, she needs to know that she cannot speak to us in that manner, and get away with it.

CAPTAIN
Good...well go on then...

RECRUIT
Me?

CAPTAIN
You're the one she thinks is her son...go on...get it out.

(RECRUIT looks confused. CAPTAIN indicates to the OFFICER who goes over to the RECRUIT and unzips his trousers.)

OFFICER
Get it out!

RECRUIT
You mean piss...in her...mouth?

CAPTAIN
Yes, piss in her mouth. Wash her filthy mouth out. We don't have to show you how to piss as well, do we?

(OFFICER holds the Prisoner's mouth open. The RECRUIT pisses into it. OFFICER forces her mouth shut so she is compelled to swallow.)

CAPTAIN
Now you filthy rutting whore you've had your refreshments…ready to sign your confession?

(Prisoner shakes her head.)

CAPTAIN
Special Policeman 467…

RECRUIT
Yes Sir…

CAPTAIN
You've been here with us over a month, haven't you?

RECRUIT
Yes Sir.

CAPTAIN
That must be hard…a young lad like you…I mean at your age mine was nearly always hard. And yours Officer?

OFFICER
Mine still is Sir.

RECRUIT
Oh I see…yes…well you know Sir.

CAPTAIN
Yes, we do 467…we do. OK, relieve yourself here.

RECRUIT
Here?

CAPTAIN
Yes, *there*…After all she's *not* your mother…is she?

RECRUIT
Definitely not Sir.

CAPTAIN
And she's a whore…
RECRUIT
Yes Sir.

CAPTAIN
Well what better opportunity to prove she's not your mother?…I mean, what

son would make his mother do that?...and you'll get some relief at the same time. One of the perks of the job, mmm?

(The CAPTAIN and OFFICER stand either side of the Prisoner. They hold her shoulders. The OFFICER forces her mouth open. The CAPTAIN bends down and whispers in her ear. She is forced to give the RECRUIT oral sex. When he has finished the three men leave the isolation cell and return to the Office. The Prisoner is left kneeling on the floor. Lights dim on her but she remains visible.)

Scene Three

(The Captain's Office.)

CAPTAIN
Well done, Special Policeman 467. You're now a full member of the special police unit. Get some glasses and the whisky out of the cupboard. Didn't take long, did it?

OFFICER
A month usually does it. You did well in there. Mind you, you can hardly call it work can you?

CAPTAIN
You'll be able to visit your family next week. Take them some presents with your first month's pay. Take your mother something nice eh? They deserve to be treated well, after all we only get one don't we.

RECRUIT
Yes Sir.

CAPTAIN
Good, well come on drink up. You deserve it. Then after, you can return the Prisoner to the Main Cell.

RECRUIT
Are you going to try to get her to sign? I mean, she might be more obliging.

OFFICER
I thought she was pretty obliging just now...gagging for it even...

CAPTAIN
No, 467. There's no point. I didn't think she'd sign, defiant one that. Go on, drink up and then take her back.

(RECRUIT leaves the Office and takes the Prisoner from the Isolation Cell to the Main Cell. The CAPTAIN and OFFICER continue drinking.)

OFFICER
And the visit?

CAPTAIN
If it happens. Can you really see them risking it? Christ they've all got too much
to lose. They'll probably be satisfied with a few well-chosen assurances from
the ambassador...

*(OFFICER moves over to the CAPTAIN holding an imaginary microphone.
They have a mock conversation as if between a reporter and the ambassador)*

OFFICER
Now tell me ambassador, how can you possibly expect your country to be
considered a suitable place for Western investment when you have such a
questionable human rights record?

CAPTAIN
The whole issue of human rights is being used as a political weapon against us.
It is being cynically politicised, yes cynically politicised, by people who
are...racist.

OFFICER
Racist?

CAPTAIN
Yes son that's what I said, racist. Racist attitudes of people who reject us from
the world market on ethnic and cultural grounds. Human rights is sacred, it
should not be used for political purposes. We have nothing to fear from
scrutiny, in fact we encourage it.

OFFICER
I see...scrutiny...even of the special police unit?

CAPTAIN
In this country our police torture no one. Our police are only carrying out their
responsibilities. In that respect they are no different from police the world over.
They are professionals and are subjected to the highest training. No, you see
people must put these vindictive rumours behind them. Ours is a safe country –
ask any of the tourists who visit us. And we have good labour practices, we
have not fallen into the trap of allowing unions to distort the minds of the work-
force. We have a cheap and willing labour force. No threat of uprisings. I ask
you, my dear fellow, can you think of a better set of conditions for safe Western
investment?

OFFICER
So it's all a conspiracy...without...

CAPTAIN
...proof. Based on rumour and conjecture. Not fact or evidence.

OFFICER
Ambassador, do you stake your reputation on that?

CAPTAIN
Of course. My reputation as a man of honour. Now I ask you, why waste precious time and effort, and of course money on tedious human rights visits? We could be using that time to forge new financial partnerships, sign lucrative contracts...Drink?
(Both men have another drink, amused at their game.)
(as himself) You've heard it a hundred times before...

OFFICER
And it always works...

CAPTAIN
Yes it's easy to convince those so eager to be convinced.

(RECRUIT re-enters room. The CAPTAIN offers him another drink.)

OFFICER
OK?

RECRUIT
Of course Sir.

CAPTAIN
Good...good. You know you should give her a name. It's a tradition, a custom of the profession. We all give a 'pet' name to our first. I called my first Feculence...

OFFICER
Mine was Guano. Still see her in the street sometimes. What'll yours be?

RECRUIT
Pus...I'll call her Pus.

OFFICER
(Laughing) Not Mother then?...Pus – that's good. You've a lot to learn 467, but you've made a good start. When you've been here a bit longer I'll really show you some tricks. Don't need any of this fancy bloody stuff we're ordering either. The most effective thing I've used was a tube of piping and a rat...

CAPTAIN
All in good time...all in good time. The boy's only just starting.

OFFICER
Yeah, OK…I'm bloody starving, nip next door and order three take-outs, chef's specials…

(The RECRUIT moves towards the OFFICER and then the CAPTAIN for money.)

CAPTAIN
Good god 467, you don't think we have to pay do you? They always come with compliments of the establishment. Just another little perk of the job.

(CAPTAIN and OFFICER continue drinking. New RECRUIT exits as the lights dim to blackout.)

Scene Four

(Main Cell.)

PRISONER 1
There's no point in you two doing it as well. One of us will be enough.

PRISONER 2
There must be another way…

PRISONER 1
No there isn't. They will just thrive if we don't try something to stop them. It's already out of hand. Once they get recognition we're finished. Something has to stop the world in its tracks. It has to be dramatic. This may do it.

PRISONER 3
But who'll know?

PRISONER 1
You must try to find an opportunity during the visit.

PRISONER 2
But what if we can't? You could die and no one will know.

PRISONER 1
But how will they explain how I died? They won't be able to erase the scars…ever…and either they will get the blame, or it will show how desperate we are to be heard.

PRISONER 2
But plenty of other people have died at their hands, and they've gotten away with it. They just lie and people are all too willing to accept their lies.

PRISONER 1
I'll make sure no one ever forgets my face. You must help me, I can't do it alone.

PRISONER 2
Shall we wait until the visit?

PRISONER 1
It may be anytime. We'll do it now, so we're ready.

(PRISONER 2 threads a needle, and slowly stitches the lips of PRISONER 1 together. She is unable to carry on. PRISONER 3 takes over from her. As the lights fade only the sound of PRISONER 1's breathing can be heard and then this also fades to silence.)

(The end.)

Part Three

The Maternal Cloister:
The Manipulation of Sor Juana?
Author's Introduction

In 1999 I was commissioned to write a play based on the life of Sor Juana Ines de la Cruz, by Theatre Carnivalesque who specialise in live performances using puppets. Here I propose to use my experience of writing the play to explore a range of cultural and artistic transactions.

In the United Kingdom Sor Juana does not have the iconic status she enjoys in the Americas and many Spanish speaking countries. In fact, not many people have even heard of her. However there is nothing particularly unusual about this. When most groups of people in my country are asked to name a famous artist the answer is invariably someone who is male, white and European.

In many ways her lack of notoriety was very liberating for me as a writer. It enabled me to try to see her as a real woman, who, through her intelligence and art, managed to survive in an oppressive, patriarchal society. Whilst still celebrating her achievements as a writer, I hoped also to explore how she might have thought and felt. It is a difficult task to try to understand someone who had such a penchant for disguises.

The difficulty of unravelling her life occurs, because to a large extent, it seems steeped in one form of manipulation or another, and is surrounded by silence. Or, as Octavio Paz states, 'of things that cannot be said' (Paz, 1988: 5).

The *details* of her life are clearly documented:
She was born in 1648, 'a daughter of the Church', meaning she was illegitimate and of humble origins. Her father was always an absent figure in her life. She left her family to live with her grandfather where her intellectual initiation took place. Due to her intellect and beauty she was a favourite at Court and particularly of the Vicerine, the Countess de Parades, Maria Luisa Manrique de Lara. As she had no desire to marry she was persuaded by her confessor, Father Antonio Nunez de Miranda, to leave the uncertainty of the Court for the safety of the Convent where she could write and learn in safety. Whilst at the convent she was befriended by the Bishop of Puebla who acted as her advisor. She incurred the wrath of Aguiar y Seijar, the Archbishop of 'New Spain', by criticising a text by Antonio de Vieryra and was punished by the removal of all her books and papers. She died in 1691 at the age of forty-six years and five months of an unknown disease contracted whilst nursing sick nuns in the convent.

It is rarely the bare detail which fascinates a writer or engages an audience. It is the motivations, opinions and machinations which history and its details can obscure. In creating a dramatic text, therefore, I wanted to use the form to both present and celebrate Sor Juana's poetry, making that poetry an integral part of the narrative: one which explores how a woman, who through her intelligence and art, attempts to survive in an oppressive patriarchal society. I was also very aware, however, of the dangers of using a through narrative, which could re-create a history that may finally justify this patriarchy. By rejecting realism in the play, I wanted to reject the illusion of realism and thus fracture the narrative structure. As Kirsten F. Nigro quotes Jeannie Forte as stating that, 'by rejecting the re-affirmation of the dominant order being in its rightful place', it is possible to 'make clear the operations of ideology' (Jeannie Forte qtd. in Nigro, 1994: 141). I wanted to destabalise an apparently stable order, 'to show the ideological seams which hold it together' (Nigro, 1994: 141).

The use of puppets was significant in breaking this illusion of realism. But I also I wanted to use the scenography as a symbolic signifier of the patriarchal society in which Sor Juana found herself. Additionally, I made the decision to conflate the characters of Father Nunez de Miranda and the Bishop of Puebla. This I felt would offer greater dramatic potential and afford richer symbolic significance.

The play begins in San Jeronimo Convent, Mexico; we are immediately presented with images of the power structures Sor Juana is contending with. The opening stage directions read as follows:

(An enclosed room with a large table surrounded by shelves of books. SOR JUANA'S puppet sits behind the table. She is very tiny and dwarfed by her surroundings. There are stars, moons and suns hanging above and around her. The stars sparkle and reveal words and letters written on them. There is an enormous three-headed puppet which hovers above her. This puppet incorporates the heads of the ARCHBISHOP – Aguiar y Seijas, the VICEROY and her FATHER – Religion, Royalty and The Patriarchal State. The puppet of the ARCHBISHOP is faceless – he is recognised by his mitre.)

This theme of power is also depicted visually in a confrontation between the Bishop of Puebla and the Archbishop. According to the historic facts the Bishop used a disguise to trick Sor Juana into writing a criticism of a piece by the Jesuit Antonio de Vieyra. It was a ploy by the Bishop to challenge the authority of the Archbishop; there was great antipathy between them. This plan failed and the Bishop's abrupt demise, which was quickly followed by his complete betrayal of Sor Juana, is shown thus:

(Shadow of the ARCHBISHOP addresses the puppeteer.)

ARCHBISHOP
Remove the disguise.

(Puppeteer removes the BISHOP'S disguise. BISHOP stands 'naked'. BISHOP begins in a panic to speak to SOR JUANA. The shadow of the

ARCHBISHOP covers the stage. As the BISHOP is speaking his cloak and mitre are lowered into the space, these are not real clothes but a solid mould. It is lowered over the BISHOP'S head; he is encased and constrained in it.)

Writing the play for puppets added a creative dimension to one of the major themes concerning Sor Juana's life: manipulation. Who is manipulating whom? To what extent are women expected not so much to change or modify, but rather invent alternatives? There is a creative and thematic tension between the puppeteers and the puppets, between the dramatic form and the content, which permits an added symbolic dimension. I wanted to use the theatrical metaphor, through puppets, to show the manipulation of women. The language itself is also steeped in symbolic significance. 'The Maternal Cloister' is also known in Spanish as the womb, and is frequently referred to as the cell. The cell-womb in which Sor Juana cloisters herself represents her complete withdrawal from the world. Paz reflects on Sor Juana, 'Reading in her cell-library-womb and in that reading is a liberation. The cloister opens to a limitless space which has a sky whose constellations are letters', (Paz, 1988: 82).
We can speculate that Sor Juana manipulated the Viceroy and the Court, the Bishop, the Archbishop and religion itself in order to retain her freedom and pursue her own desires for learning and writing. But there is also the implication that, due to their position in such a patriarchal society, the Bishop and the Archbishop were ultimately the more successful manipulators. At the end of the play when Sor Juana has been abandoned by the Countess and betrayed by the Bishop, she is compelled to renounce her writing and forced to sign a confession, in her own blood. The violence of this act, both morally and physically, is dramatically represented by the use of puppets:

(SOR JUANA'S puppet moves around the empty room, the shelves continue to move in. The space becomes increasingly more restricted.)

SOR JUANA
My state. The state I now find myself in.
All my caution and cleverness, but still...here I am.
I have lost all my protectors. Those I loved and trusted have abandoned me.

(The three-headed puppet reappears. It bears down on her and speaks.)

PUPPET
You have dedicated your life to secular writing and philosophical criticisms.

You have neglected the sacred.
You must confess to this and disown your moral, your witty and your amorous poems. Your plays, your letters – in effect your entire work.

(As the multi-headed puppet speaks these lines, rolls of paper are pulled from the body of SOR JUANA by her puppeteer. Throughout the next exchange SOR JUANA is lifted, she is swung around and dropped on the floor. After she has signed the confession the three-headed puppet leaves. The bookshelves move in closer, further constraining SOR JUANA. Her puppet remains 'broken' centre-stage.)

Kirsten F. Nigro's chapter, 'Inventions and Transgressions', in Negotiating Performance, makes some interesting points in her analysis of The Eternal Feminine, a play written by Rosario Castellanos in 1973, and which has amongst its characters Sor Juana. She believes that gender is simultaneously representation and self-representation. She suggests that, in Castellanos' terms, women may be required not so much to change or modify, but rather invent alternatives. One of her characters says, 'It isn't enough to discover who we are. We have to invent ourselves' (Castellanos qtd. in Nigro, 1994: 144).

This is a fascinating idea for a writer who is about to write a play about Sor Juana. She clearly discovered herself, and out of necessity invented and reinvented herself. My task was really exactly the same. Using Octavio Paz's seminal work on Sor Juana and her own writing, I had to discover who I

The University of Plymouth production of The Maternal Cloister, May 2002.

thought she was and then reinvent her for a theatrical performance which would have a resonance for contemporary audiences. For me the essential theme of her story is power and the exertion of it. It is within this over-arching theme we see the importance of her struggle and the range of transgressions she was willing to commit as a woman and artist. Because of these her life was one of danger and careful negotiation or invention.

We can see evidence of the range of transgressions in her writing, which I integrated into the text alongside my own words. This not only gave the play a fractured narrative structure, but also celebrated her contemporary significance as a feminist, and as an artist, through her poetry. One of her major transgressions is her desire for learning and knowledge. These were the domains of the male:

> SOR JUANA
> If there is nothing inside the head I will have nothing on the outside. Cut the hair. Remove the Cheese!
> Oh yes it is a well-known fact cheese clogs the mind, cloying and thick.
> Such an easy abstention.
> The mind must be free to grow, unfettered.
> To soar.

She not only had a yearning for religious enquiry, which would have been acceptable within the confines of the Convent, but showed an avid interest in the sciences and astronomy. These were the acceptable power images within her society but were related to books and men, which through her interest as a woman she challenged:

> SOR JUANA
> Foolish, you men – so very skilled
> At wrongly blaming womankind,
> Not seeing you're alone at fault
> For the wrongs you plan in woman's mind…
> No woman, with you can hope to score;
> Whatever she does, she's bound to fail;
> Rejecting you, she's ungrateful –
> Yielding, you call her lewd.

Her relationship with the Countess, which many have cited as lesbian in nature, can also be seen as a social transgression. Within the play I use the exchanges between Sor Juana and the Countess to not only acknowledge this possible attraction, but also to develop the themes of the precariousness of Sor Juana's position. She is socially dependent on the patronage of the Countess. The relationship illuminates many things: the vulnerability of Sor Juana both socially and possibly sexually; the power exerted over her by society; and, because of this her need to write, 'surrounded by silence' (Paz, 1988: 5):

SOR JUANA
It is so in my affection
And more that I cannot impart;
But you should know all that I cannot say,
And know that love beyond expression.

As well as acknowledging Sor Juana as an artist, I also wanted to use her experiences to interrogate attitudes towards women, both on stage and in real-life recognizing, as in Jesusa Rodriguez's work *Corpus Delecti*, that in performance the body is never taken value-free. I feel that working with puppets can subvert this.

As Elin Diamond in *Unmaking Mimesis* states, 'the decentered subject implies the dismantling of the self-reflecting cogito-self, whose inferior other has been traditionally gendered female' (Diamond, 1997: vii). The surreal use of the Sor Juana puppet enables a distancing by the spectator. The action is witnessed and understood through a complex range of signs. She herself becomes a sign. As Paz notes, we witness her life as a series of choices, imposed by necessity that she adopts with open eyes. When we see Sor Juana manipulating her circumstances we applaud her intelligence, resilience and pragmatism. When we witness those very circumstances being manipulated by others, we recognize the vulnerability of her position and admire her more.

Double standards on our part? I don't think so, just an increasing awareness of the gross imbalance and misuse of power in society. Through the range of theatrical signifiers used in the play we recognise her importance as a woman, but are distanced from a simplistic identification with her. We can recognise her defeat without categorising her in the role of female victim. Politically I think it's important to recognize her ultimate defeat, but I wanted to make the distinction between being defeated and being a victim. At the end of the play Sor Juana's puppet not only is de-centered, but literally disembodied. After she has been left 'broken' centre-stage, she physically rises above the constraints and machinations of the Church, and using her own words gives a savage indictment on her society:

(Shadows of the ARCHBISHOP and BISHOP appear. They dominate the stage. SOR JUANA'S head becomes gradually disembodied and begins to rise, until she is finally clear of the shadow and soars above the room amongst the stars, moons and suns.)

SOR JUANA
What concern have you, world, in persecuting me?
Why do I offend you, when all I desire
Is to give splendour to my mind
And not my mind to splendid things?

I do not care for possessions or wealth,

Being more content
To endow my mind with treasures,
Rather than treasures with my mind.

And I esteem not appearance, which age
Removes in civil stealth.
You see, I am not impressed by wealth.
I believe in the truth that
the vanities of life are the better to expend
Than a life expended in vanities.

The only thing I feel Sor Juana has become a victim of is the array of labels placed upon her: lesbian; feminist; muse; goddess; heroine; manipulator. I'm not sure in the end these are particularly useful. Perhaps we should see her as an example of a woman, a fine artist, who in very difficult circumstances struggled to survive, and to a large extent achieved that struggle. But one who was finally overwhelmed by structures too powerful to fight. In this sense as Nigro points out, 'the effects of power that women experience on a personal level are political acts, which is to significantly redefine the nature of the political' (Nigro, 1994: 155).

I feel that these themes, although particular to Sor Juana and her culture, also have a universality which speaks to different generations and cultures. So I would hope that an audience at *The Maternal Cloister* would ask: what have we done, and what are we doing, to dismantle those hierarchical structures and to redress such an imbalance of power?

Works Cited

Diamond, E. (1997) *Unmaking Mimesis*. London: Routledge.

Nigro, K. F. (1994) 'Inventions and Transgressions' in D. Taylor & J. Villegas (eds.), *Negotiating Performance*. Durham and London: Duke University Press.

Paz, O. (1988) *Sor Juana, Or The Traps of Faith*. Trans. M. Sayers Peden. Cambridge, Mass.: The Belknap Press of Harvard University Press.

Sor Juana Ines de la Cruz (1985) *Sor Juana Ines de la Cruz. Poems. A Bilingual Anthology*. Trans. M. Sayers Peden. Arizona, USA: Bilingual Press/Editorial Bilingue.

The Maternal Cloister

The Maternal Cloister was first performed by Lusty Juventus as a rehearsed reading at I Encontro de Performance e Politica nas Americas in Rio de Janeiro, Brazil, July 2000, with the following cast: Ruth Way, David Coslett and Roberta Mock. Directed by Christine Roberts and Cariad Astles.

The first full-scale production was performed by second year undergraduates studying 'Political Theatre' at the University of Plymouth in May 2002. Due to the size of the cast, some modifications were made to the script and some parts were played by more than one actor (for example, there were five different people representing various facets of Sor Juana). The cast was as follows: Anna Bell (Sor Juana); Helen Duffy (Sor Juana); Georgina Hill (Sor Juana); Anne Jillings (three headed structure); Anna Leavy (nun); Kate Lines (Sor Juana); Paula Main (Sor Juana, court dancer); Daniel Marshall (Bishop of Puebla); Emily Maxwell (The Vicereine); Martin Rowe (Bishop of Puebla); Claire Rule (nun); Joanne Sanders (Bishop of Puebla); Jennifer Schmidt (nun, court dancer); Kathryn Seymour (nun, court dancer) and Hannah Wierzbicki (nun, court dancer).

Directed by Christine Roberts. Lighting by Cyril Squire and Kristof Talikowski. Costumes constructed and sound operated by Terri Toohey. Construction of puppets and props members of the cast and Danielle Fenemore, Sarah Irish and Amy Penn. Music by Oliver Chapman, Helen Duffy, Laura Dillon and Emily Palmer.

The Characters

Sor Juana Ines de la Cruz (Seventeenth Century Mexican Nun)
Three headed power structure representing:
Aguiar y Seijas (Archbishop of 'New Spain')
Pedro Manuel de Asbaje y Vargas Machuca (Sor Juana's Father)
Marquis de la Laguna, Tomas de la Cerda (Viceroy of Mexico)

Marquis de la Laguna, Tomas de la Cerda (Viceroy of Mexico)
The Countess de Parades, Maria Luisa Manrique de Lara (Vicereine of Mexico)
Father Antonio Nunez de Miranda/Bishop of Puebla (Two separate people, conflated into one character)
Nuns and Court Dancers

Scene One

(An enclosed room with a large table surrounded by shelves of books. SOR JUANA'S puppet sits behind the table. She is very tiny and dwarfed by her surroundings. There are stars, moons and suns hanging above and around her.

113

The stars sparkle and reveal words and letters written on them. There is an enormous three-headed puppet which hovers above her. This puppet incorporates the heads of the ARCHBISHOP – Aguiar y Seijas, the VICEROY and her FATHER – Religion, Royalty and The Patriarchal State. SOR JUANA'S arms flail around her.
The puppet of the ARCHBISHOP is faceless. This is also the case when the puppet of the BISHOP appears. They are recognized by the mitres/hats they wear.
SOR JUANA stands and moves forward. She addresses the audience directly.)

SOR JUANA
My name is Sor Juana Ines de la Cruz. I was born on 2 December 1648, Juana de Asbaje y Ramirez in San Miguel de Nepantla, Mexico. Ines daughter of the Church, a term used when recording an illegitimate birth. So I was illegitimate – not greatly important in those days but it became so as I was to rise in society and mix in the highest circles.

I was born where solar rays
Stared down at me from overhead,
Not squint-eyed, as in other climates.

My mother, a criolla, Dona Isabel Ramirez de Santillana,
A mother of six children, five female and one male – all illegitimate.
She had many love affairs.
Men loved her as they were also to love me,
But where she received, I rejected.

My father Pedro Manuel de Asbaje y Vargas Machuca – a Basque.
Who was he? What became of his family?
Pedro Manuel de Asbaje remained in the shadows. He was a disembodied man.
A ghost.

To be the child of a man with no honour
Would be a blight I had to own.
If my essence was given by no other,
I had not known it was his alone.
Unlike my mother's munificence,
When considering your heritage,
Offering many a likely patriarch
From whom to choose your ancestry?

The notable pedigree of my family was not to be found in the men, but in the women who all showed independence, fortitude and energy! What spirit! What courage!
None could read, but all could fight.
My fight took a different course – but the battle would be as bloody
And also fought to the death!

You think that by choosing to enter the convent of San Jeronimo
I ran away? Took the easy option?
I had many friends at court, particularly the Countess.
We loved each other very deeply. But my position had always been a tenuous one.
The pursuit of knowledge was always my greatest concern. Through learning you can gain liberation.
This was offered to me by my other great supporter Father Antonio Nunez de Miranda, the Bishop of Puebla. He convinced me it was the right move for me to make. Through the Bishop and the Countess I have achieved great success as a writer, and more freedom as a woman than can be imagined. Through their friendship I have also secured the goodwill of Aguiar y Seijas – the Archbishop himself. Renowned for his piety, his power, his hatred of women.

(The three-headed puppet becomes more apparent.)

ARCHBISHOP
God favours us with his indifference!

The University of Plymouth production of The Maternal Cloister, *May 2002.*

SOR JUANA
The perfect state is only achieved when one loves without hope of having that love returned.

FATHER
You are a daughter of the church...

ARCHBISHOP
Illegitimate.

VICEROY
With only me as your protector.

SOR JUANA
To be the child of a man with no honour
Would be a blight I had to own.
If my essence was given by no other
I had not known it was his alone.
So it is then...alone.

(SOR JUANA waves her arms and the large puppet disappears.)

SOR JUANA
Ever since my childhood.

(SOR JUANA'S puppet slumps on the floor. As she sits there books begin to fall from the shelves and land around her. She opens the books, slowly to begin with, and then she stands and moves around the shelves. Books still fall around her; she begins to read from the books, trying to memorise passages. When she fails she instructs her puppeteer to cut off some of her hair.)

SOR JUANA
No head should be adorned with hair and naked of learning. Cut it...cut more!

(SOR JUANA can be heard muttering passages from the books and when she fails to remember, she demands more of her hair be cut. The hair continues to grow.)

If there is nothing inside I will have nothing on the outside. Cut the hair. Remove the cheese! Oh yes, it is a well-known fact cheese clogs the mind, cloying and thick. Such an easy abstention. The mind must be free to grow, unfettered. To soar.

(She then rises into the air and begins to study the letters on the stars. The FATHER puppet enters and looks up at her. She slowly turns from the stars to gaze down on him.)

SOR JUANA
Father...your evasive figure too readily escaped me,
And though to my embrace you are forever absent,
You are trapped in my fantasy.

SOR JUANA'S PUPPETEER TO SOR JUANA
The absent person, the figure in the shadows at night. We project whatever we
want onto the person who is missing. Onto the person we have missed. We
project our desires, our hatred and our fears.

SOR JUANA
Absence is a vacuum which I can fill with my imagination.
I have seen too clearly what can happen to women who live only through their
men. The abandonment of sanity and dignity. The near madness which can grip
a woman in love...or lust. Abandonment of everything.
Until that very resignation causes the object of desire to recoil.
Leaving the woman alone in her abandonment.
Abandoned.

*(Both puppet of SOR JUANA and the FATHER meet. He wraps himself around
her and then leaves. She searches the space for him, but is clearly alone. She
returns to the books on the floor, and begins to move her arms as if writing. As
she does this her arms get gradually longer.)*

Scene Two

*(Music to indicate The Court. This should also reflect Mexico and be lively and
flirtatious. Faces look through the gaps in the shelves, and over the music a
collection of their opinions and comments can be heard. Throughout the music
and voices SOR JUANA'S puppet and a person perform a dance together which
indicates SOR JUANA'S desire for admiration, her coquettishness, but also her
ability to manipulate her position at the Court.)*

VOICES
She is the target of all eyes, admired, the centre of attention.
What wit.
What cleverness.
Is it innate or acquired?
Elegance of face and bearing.
What conceit.
What desire for adulation and flattery.
In one so ill-connected.
Her status at this court is brilliant.
Her status...not her situation.
No name. No rank. No fortune.
What patronage – the Vicereine clearly adores her. What luck.She plays a

dangerous game.
She dare not refuse absolutely...
Yet must refuse whilst still fuelling the fire.

No name, or rank or dowry
She has only her wit.
She lives by her wits.
She excels in the art of flattery.
She has learned to manipulate with skill.

(Exit person with whom SOR JUANA has been dancing.)

SOR JUANA
Amid such excessive praise,
With my attention desired by all
In all the assembly I could not find
In my esteem a worthy partner;
And so, adored by so many,
I refused all to my heart.

I have no name, or fortune or father. I am the Lady in Waiting to the Vicereine, but viceroys have their posting for only a few years and then leave, never to return.

SOR JUANA'S PUPPETEER
The world designed to exploit dependence and patronage is a dangerous place to be for one lacking power, position, name or dowry.
(SOR JUANA'S puppet sits whilst her puppeteer begins to place the books back on the shelves. The puppeteer becomes the BISHOP of Puebla and talks to SOR JUANA as he continues to block out the faces with the books.)

BISHOP
As Bishop of Puebla I can be of great support to you. This life you are leading here is really based on a myth. You cannot hope to gain a successful marriage without a dowry. Do you want to marry? You hate domestic life. You have a complete dislike of the thought of hearth and home. It's true. I know it.

SOR JUANA
I have always yearned for knowledge, this has been my main desire. In achieving knowledge and learning I can really find liberation and a true sense of freedom. Owned by no one. Dependent only on myself. Responsible to no one but myself. No husband or child, or any kind of physical love...can this really be the true desire? Will it really be a complete fulfillment? Will it be enough?

(As The BISHOP continues to speak to SOR JUANA he is joined by the other puppeteer, also in religious clothes. One begins to surround SOR JUANA with

118

candles, whilst the other pulls the shelves in towards her, restricting the space in which she can move.)

BISHOP
I can help you escape from this inhospitable world. I will light the altar candles as you take the veil. Enter the cell, the Mother's Womb, the Maternal Cloister – and you will be safe in my friendship, support and protection.

(The BISHOP now becomes SOR JUANA'S puppeteer. He whispers in her ear and coaxes her. The other person places an enormous veil over SOR JUANA'S head, it completely covers her body and is reminiscent of a shroud. The BISHOP then addresses the audience as this happens.)

BISHOP
Fishers of souls are awesome because they are also seducers.

(As he says this SOR JUANA'S arms reach up towards the letter/stars and manage to touch some of them.)

Scene Three

(PUPPETEER 1 holds a multi-charactered puppet. These represent many nuns. He has the BISHOP'S 'hat' on. He is speaking to the PUPPETEER 2 who has the ARCHBISHOP'S 'hat' on. The puppet of nuns appears nervous and embarrassed.)

PUPPETEER 1/BISHOP
Your holiness, I have brought them here, before you, as you required.

(ARCHBISHOP recoils.)

PUPPETEER 2/ARCHBISHOP
Not so close – you know how much I hate being in the presence of *them*.

PUPPETEER 1
Who?

PUPPETEER 2
(Whispers) Women.

PUPPETEER 1
But these are vessels of God. These do not count as real women. If we are to continue with your plan Archbishop, we have to use women.

PUPPETEER 2
I tell you Father Antonio, I have not been this close to the defected breed for

many years...

PUPPETEER 1
I know...

PUPPETEER 2
No woman is permitted inside my house.

PUPPETEER 1
I know...

PUPPETEER 2
And that if I so much as hear of a woman entering my house I would order the very bricks she has stepped on to be removed.

PUPPETEER 1
I know...but I am holding them high your holiness. Their feet are not touching the floor. They will not touch you, but I cannot do this alone. Would you like me to hold the bowl, and you hold the women? *(ARCHBISHOP looks horrified)* No, no of course not.

(PUPPETEER 2 holds out a bowl beneath the nuns. He has an expression of disgust on his face. PUPPETEER 1 presses the backs of the nuns' puppet and water falls from underneath their habits.)

PUPPETEER 1
Are you sure of the value of this?

PUPPETEER 2
Absolutely certain. Do you think I would subject myself to this if there were any doubt?

PUPPETEER 1
And it is profitable?

PUPPETEER 2
Of course...Immensely. Childless women will pay anything to increase their fertility. We owe it to them as God's servants. But it is our little secret. You understand?

PUPPETEER 1
Yes, yes...But why nuns' urine, in particular?

PUPPETEER 2
Their purity...their innocence...their lack of...use. Packed with fertile hormones. One mouthful and I guarantee it would make even you fertile.

PUPPETEER 1
As in all other things your holiness, I am abstemious.

PUPPETEER 2
You couldn't afford it anyway.
Never be foolish enough to forget your position Father Antonio.
You are after all only the Bishop of Puebla, Mexico.
I am the Archbishop of the New Spain.
You retain power only until I choose to let you.
Power is not an absolute. It is taken or given. It can just as easily be taken away.
In your arrogance I would hate you to forget this.

(PUPPETEER 2 exits.)

PUPPETEER 1
Don't worry your holiness I won't. Oh no I certainly won't.
(As they exit SOR JUANA'S puppet, wearing a smaller veil, enters over their heads.)

SOR JUANA
Disenchantment,
This is my fate.
With proof you're rightly named
The end of illusion.
I could lose all,
Yet this is not my only claim
Far greater is that of being undeceived.

And so my way will be one of care and caution.
The fine line beckons before me, but has to be travelled.

Scene Four

(Puppeteer becomes SOR JUANA and manipulates two puppets. One represents Royalty and is the VICEREINE, The Countess de Paredes. The other represents the Church and is The BISHOP. Overseeing all of this is an image of the ARCHBISHOP.)

COUNTESS TO PUPPETEER AS SOR JUANA
I cannot overstate the truth, beloved one,
When I am not with you,
Even my words seem a fabrication

SOR JUANA
So although I would call you mine

I cannot expect
That mine you should be thought,
Only as yours I would wish to be seen.

BISHOP
Such audacious expressions of affection ensure your position at Court. This must be encouraged. We will all benefit from gaining the confidences of the Viceroy and Vicereine. We will continue to pay for whatever gifts you may bestow on them.

SOR JUANA
On one hand I serve the Convent and, on the other, the Court. My position at the Court strengthens my position at the Convent. Only through such actions can I gain any form of independence.

ARCHBISHOP
The manipulator manipulates the manipulator! I could learn a lot from this woman. The Bishop is a fool who has neither the courage nor the wit to withhold me for long. The Vicereine will soon leave and die…Enjoy your position Sor Juana, for as in all things it is only temporary. There is no permanence.

BISHOP
Rumours will of course fly, 'such expressions of love and between two women'. But love it seems to be. And who am I to stand in the way?

SOR JUANA
Two hundred pesos please for the publication of 'Allegorical Neptune'.

BISHOP
Any time my dear, any time. Whatever it takes to keep them sweet.

ARCHBISHOP
Any time…my dear…any time. Your time little lady is running out.

COUNTESS
I am in such delirium,
In the warmth of your love
That, even imagined, your merest request
Will drive me to madness.

SOR JUANA
It is so in my affection
And more that I cannot impart;
But you should know all that I cannot say
And know that love beyond expression.

(The two puppets begin to fill the room with objects: shells; musical instruments; mathematical instruments; astronomical instruments; more books; paintings; magnifying glasses; telescopes etc. until the room is full. The puppeteer exits. The puppet of SOR JUANA enters. She sits amongst the objects studying the stars and the sky. The puppeteer enters as The ARCHBISHOP manipulating a puppet of the COUNTESS.)

ARCHBISHOP TO AUDIENCE
The Countess de Paredes, Maria Luisa Manrique de Lara and her husband, the Marquis de la Laguna governed Mexico or New Spain, as I like to call it, for six years. They assumed office on 7 November 1680 and relinquished it on 30 November 1686. The couple left the city and a great number of coaches accompanied them.

SOR JUANA
To leave and to remain, departing without taking.

COUNTESS
To leave behind a soul, but another one to take.

SOR JUANA
Souls do not possess a sex.

COUNTESS
My devotion will not cease with separation.

ARCHBISHOP
Alone, always alone.
The fates can be very cruel can't they? But these events must be used and exploited for the correct balance of things to be maintained.
On 22 April 1693 the most crushing of news came from Spain. It was very unexpected and rendered the rebellious nun even more vulnerable. Tomas de la Cerda, Marquis de la Laguna, died suddenly. His widow, the nun's beloved Countess, grief-stricken and in mourning had to adapt to her new situation.

COUNTESS
I could no longer concern myself with the nun in San Jeronimo Convent, Mexico, or with the problems that she was soon to find herself embroiled in.

ARCHBISHOP
And in choosing to place her faith in the friendship of the Bishop, Father Nunez de Miranda, Sor Juana made her final and fatal mistake.

(COUNTESS puppet is replaced by BISHOP puppet – still manipulated by ARCHBISHOP.)

SOR JUANA
Burst forth, rising grief,
Break all bridges
By the torrent of tears
Carried on the wave's crest.

(BISHOP moves towards SOR JUANA.)

SOR JUANA
Alone, always alone.

BISHOP
Confess your doubts to the only one who knows.
I am your confessor. I know your true passion has been learning.
I have minimized the conflict between religious life and a life dedicated to
study and writing.
How can you forget that I was the one who persuaded you to choose the path of
religion? That on the day you took the veil, I myself lit the altar candles.
You need not feel alone. Or fear your helpless position.
I am all the security you need.
I am, after all, The Inquisitor.

SOR JUANA
My confessor. My father.
A man who specialises in detecting heresy and sins against the Church.
My security…
Hands tightly intertwined,
Palm on palm laid,
With gestures they can say
What mouths must leave unsaid.

Scene Five

*(SOR JUANA stands and moves forward. The BISHOP recedes into the
shadows. SOR JUANA directly addresses the audience.*
*During this speech shadows of the ARCHBISHOP and the women appear
behind SOR JUANA.)*

SOR JUANA
During the siege of 1692 a procession of fifty women went to the palace of the
Archbishop. Their complaint? 'That not only were they not given maize for
their sustenance in return for their money, but the guards had beaten a poor
woman and made her miscarry'.
The Archbishop, Aguiar y Seijas, did not allow them to enter. He proudly
announced that, 'no woman had entered since I the venerable prelate, have
taken up residence.'

The riot grew and a most unexpected thing happened – it strengthened Aguiar y Seijas' position. He thought he was invincible, and in thinking it, became so. These are the circumstances through which I have lived, through which I have had to cautiously, skillfully, find my way.

I make my utterances in the most dangerous of circumstance, do not think that I am not aware that these utterances are surrounded by silence. The silence of things that cannot be said.

But do not think for one moment that I have ever been manipulated.

I know exactly what I am doing.

Look at me. At my wealth, my books, my ability to learn and study, observe my fame.

I have fought a bloody battle to reach for the sky, and in so doing have made the stars my own.

My freedom is not a physical one, but neither are my constraints.

(SOR JUANA'S puppet soars into the air and writes among the stars.)

What are those magical elements
Of the mystical Indians
Of my home, whose spells spread,
Spilling out through all the words of my pen?

Scene Six

(ARCHBISHOP'S shadow covers stage. His voice is heard – possibly amplified? During this there is a solar eclipse. All light is blotted out.)

ARCHBISHOP
During the summer of 1691 it rained incessantly in the Valley of Mexico. The crops were ruined and the capital was flooded. No one could enter the city and there was a shortage of coal, firewood, fruit, vegetables, fowl and all that comes from outside the city. Many adobe houses collapsed and for several weeks the city was a lake. On 23 August there was a solar eclipse, and the people believed that its malign influence was the cause of a new calamity. The Viceroy did what all indecisive governments do – hold meetings.

Power shifted from them to me.

Things were never to be the same again...particularly for Sor Juana Ines de la Cruz.
That abomination – that nun,
Who instead of scourging herself, wrote plays and poems.

Little did she know that her light was also about to be eclipsed.

Scene Seven

(BISHOP visiting SOR JUANA in her room. He is reading one of her poems.)

BISHOP
As always Sor Juana, excellent. You know how much I admire your work.

SOR JUANA
Of course, you are my true and constant friend.

BISHOP
Unfortunately I cannot fund this for publication.

SOR JUANA
Why not? You have already said you think it is good – and I know there are people who will want to read it.

BISHOP
It is not your talent or your fame I am concerned about! It is your safety. With the Viceroy and Vicereine no longer able to offer you protection, and with the rise of the Archbishop's influence you are in a dangerous position. He despises the fact that you spend your time writing plays and poems about love and philosophy and not about religion. He has a point my dear. You are, after all, a nun.

SOR JUANA
Does he question my belief?

BISHOP
I'm not sure…

SOR JUANA
Do you?

BISHOP
Of course not.

SOR JUANA
Well then couldn't you inform him, convince him of my piety?

BISHOP
You know the feeling of dislike and distrust between the Archbishop and myself. You cannot expect me to place myself in such a position. It would be too dangerous and ultimately I don't think it would work in your favour.

SOR JUANA
Then what can I do?

BISHOP
Take my advice, for once in your life my dear, listen to what I have to say. If you insist on continuing your writing…

SOR JUANA
And I do…

BISHOP
Yes I thought you would…well, concern yourself more with writing about religion…about Christ…about God. Look you could combine your love of philosophy with an exploration of religion. Why not write a critique of the Jesuit Antonio de Vieyra's sermon 'In Defence of Heraclitus'? You have after all spent many years analysing the nature of unreciprocated love.

SOR JUANA
And you feel sure this will place me in a favourable light with the Archbishop?

BISHOP
You have my word on it.

(Shadow of ARCHBISHOP appears. SOR JUANA begins to search the bookshelves for a book she finds the one she wants and begins to read. She is unaware of the BISHOP and the ARCHBISHOP).

ARCHBISHOP
You realize that she will attack what Vieyra writes?

BISHOP
Not necessarily, she must take my advice in all matters. You see, yours is not the only position of power.

ARCHBISHOP
You realise if she does attack him it will be an oblique attack on me, an attack I will not countenance. It will be seen as a confrontation with the Jesuit friend of the Archbishop. What can your motive be in this venture? You know you are putting her at risk. Are you using her to attack me? Or to feed your arrogance?

BISHOP
She will be safe as long as she takes my advice.

(BISHOP exits and ARCHBISHOP'S shadow dims.)

Scene Eight

(Puppet of SOR JUANA frantically writing. Reams of paper float down and fill the stage. Multi-puppet of other nuns collect and read these. They are very

disapproving. They mutter some of the contents of the writing.)

NUNS
My own view is that Christ did wish that his love be returned.
I confront Vieyra's opinion that Christ did not wish his love to be returned for his own sake but for man's sake.

(NUNS exit. BISHOP disguised as SOR FILOTEA enters and tries to catch the sheets of paper which SOR JUANA is still writing on. The shadow of the ARCHBISHOP fills the back of the stage area. He is a constant and ominous presence. Throughout all this there are snatches of conversation between SOR JUANA and SOR FILOTEA. SOR JUANA is indicating what she is writing and SOR FILOTEA is commenting on it.)

BISHOP
In my opinion Vieyra wandered some distance from this point, for he misunderstood and stated the opposite; seeing a selfless Christ, he persuaded himself that Christ did not desire his love to be requited.
These are important opinions Sor Juana, you will need my help in having them published.

SOR JUANA
The lover makes requited love a means to his end; Christ makes reciprocation a means to man's well-being.

BISHOP
I will be responsible for the prologue, brief though it will be, and will sign it Sor Filotea, a nun of Puebla and student of the poet Sor Juana.

SOR JUANA
I do not agree that St. Augustine's vision of the fall of man is founded in predestination, and the idea of 'negative favours'. Negative favours do not negate free will; they augment it.

BISHOP
At last Sor Juana you are concerning yourself with the book of Christ. You have spent much time in the study of philosophers and poets; now it is well for you to better your occupation with concerns of God, not secularism.

SOR JUANA
I do not know how to express my gratitude for your immeasurable kindness in publishing my scribblings, Sor Filotea.

ARCHBISHOP
You give foolish advice, Sor Filotea. If you think you can belittle me and my position by the writings of this nun, you are very mistaken. You have chosen the wrong side on which to fight.

(ARCHBISHOP to the puppeteer.)
Remove the disguise.
(Puppeteer removes the BISHOP'S disguise. BISHOP stands 'naked'.)
How does it feel to stand alone Antonio Nunez? Stripped to the...essentials?

BISHOP
Father Antonio Nunez de Miranda, Bishop of Puebla.

ARCHBISHOP
You have chosen the wrong side on which to fight. Have you also forgotten my advice about power? Surely you are not that stupid.

(BISHOP in a panic begins to speak to SOR JUANA. He is still aware of the Archbishop.)

BISHOP
Sor Juana, temper your criticism. Renounce your attack. You are attracting the very worst attention. You cannot afford to make an enemy of the Archbishop. You must take my advice Sor Juana. I will be powerless to help you against the Archbishop. Take my advice. Obey me in this matter.

SOR JUANA
I believe in the truth that
The vanities of life are the better to expend
Than a life expended in vanities.

BISHOP
You have always been willful Sor Juana...

SOR JUANA
You encouraged me. I was following your advice in choosing this sermon. Why did you make such a suggestion if only to tell me to withdraw my opinions?

BISHOP
Obey me in this matter Sor Juana. Beg forgiveness for your sins.

(As the BISHOP is speaking his cloak and hat are lowered into the space. These are not real clothes but a mould. It is lowered over the BISHOP'S head, he is encased in it.)

SOR JUANA
Writing my opinions with clarity and truthfulness is not a sin and I am sorry Father but I will never beg forgiveness, not from you or the Archbishop.

ARCHBISHOP
And so my instincts were correct all along. I see in this Sor Juana an example

of perdition and dissoluteness. Instead of scourging herself she wastes her time either attacking me or in writing poems and plays. See to it Sor Filotea, Bishop of Puebla.

(BISHOP bows to the ARCHBISHOP and extracts his arms out from the mould to pull the Puppet of SOR JUANA down from the 'sky'.)

BISHOP
I have warned you Sor Juana of your vanity and rebelliousness. I have warned you of the very serious risk for educated women, that the pride and power they feel education will give them, will lead them from their natural state of obedience. You are in serious danger Sor Juana. Do not expect our long-standing friendship to protect you now. And with the Countess removed, you would do well to heed my advice and seek the favour of Aguiar y Seijas, The Archbishop.

SOR JUANA
But Nunez de Miranda, you, you who persuaded me to take the veil. You, who lit the altar candles when I took my vows. You who encouraged my writing and my challenge of Vieya's sermon. You knew it would anger the Archbishop and still you persuaded me in my actions. You fed my rebelliousness and exploited my fame. And yet you now desert me.....for your own safety.

BISHOP
And for your own Sor Juana. You are without protection.

SOR JUANA
Betrayal is a bitter blow Father. I am now at the mercy of the Holy Office.

(SOR JUANA pulls away from the grip of the BISHOP and flies above him and amongst the ARCHBISHOP'S shadow.)

SOR JUANA
Foolish, you men – so very skilled
At wrongly blaming womankind,
Not seeing you're alone at fault
For wrongs you plant in woman's mind.
After you win by urgent plea
The right to taint her good name,
You still expect her to behave –
You, that persuade her into shame.
You break her resistance down
And then, all righteousness, announce
That the trifling of women
And not your persistence, is to blame.
No woman, with you, can hope to score;
Whatever she does, she's bound to fail;

The University of Plymouth production of The Maternal Cloister, *May 2002.*

Rejecting you, she's ungrateful –
Yielding, you call her lewd.
I understand well enough what powerful weapons
You use in pressing for evil;
Your insolence is allied
With the world, the flesh, and the devil!

BISHOP
I know I am right. I know no doubt. I condemn to hell all those who oppose my opinions.

ARCHBISHOP
We are not so very dissimilar Father. And now it falls to you to deal with this woman. You who offered her the opportunity to escape from the dangers of the outside world, must now make sure she stays completely locked away from it. Deny her right to her letters, her writing and remove all her books.

SOR JUANA
So it was all a sham. The love and care and kindness. Empty and without substance.

(SOR JUANA returns from the 'sky' to the room. The possessions and books etc. are removed. She is left alone. The stage is very bare.)

Scene Nine

(SOR JUANA'S puppeteer speaks to audience. SOR JUANA puppet moves around the empty room, the shelves continue to move in, the space becomes more restricted.)

PUPPETEER
We now live in a world where change is commonplace, encouraged. We move from one city to another, one country to another. We often have many different careers in life, many different lovers, or friends. For those of us used to living like this it is hard to understand the life of Sor Juana. Abandoned and unprotected; intelligent and spirited. Did she ever regret the choices she made? Did she ever long for a life which offered more adventure, or excitement, or passion? Or, dare I say it? More danger?

SOR JUANA
…Were there one so daring, one so brave
That regardless of the danger he might place
Upon Apollo's reins, fearless hand
Guiding the fleeting chariot bathed in gold.
The variety of life he would desire,
Rejecting a state to last his span.

My state. The state I now find myself in.
All my caution and cleverness, but still…here I am.
I have lost all my protectors. Those I loved and trusted have abandoned me.

(SOR JUANA becomes increasingly fearful and agitated.)

I have everything to lose. Heresy against the church…the Inquisition.

(The three-headed puppet of Religion, Patriarchy and State reappears. It beasr down on her.)

PUPPET
You have dedicated your life to secular writing and philosophical criticisms. You have neglected the sacred. You must confess to this and disown your moral and your witty and your amorous poems. Your plays, your letters….in effect your entire work.

(As the multi-headed puppet speaks these lines, rolls of paper are pulled from the body of SOR JUANA.)

Do you agree to forsake your writing of poems and plays?
Your love of learning?
Do you confess that your sins are great and without equal?
That you deserve to be condemned to eternal death in infinite hells?

(Throughout this SOR JUANA is lifted, swung around and dropped on the floor.)

SOR JUANA
I confess...

PUPPET
Confess what? What do you admit?

SOR JUANA
I confess that for many years I have lived in religion, without religion.

PUPPET
If not worse that a pagan might live?

SOR JUANA
Yes...

PUPPET
That it is your will to renew your vows and pass a year seeking *our* approval?

SOR JUANA
Yes...I entreat that my previous life be considered as never having existed and I promise a new and truly religious life.

PUPPET
Sign...with your blood.

(A document is presented. SOR JUANA'S body is ripped as she confesses and signs. She speaks the confession in Spanish, the PUPPET simultaneously in English.)

SOR JUANA
Docta explicacion del misterio, y voto que hizo de defender la Purisima Concepcion de Nuestra Senora, la madre Juana Ines de la Cruz.

PUPPET
Learned Explication of the Mystery, and Vow Made by Sister Juana Ines de la Cruz to Defend the Immaculate Conception of Our Lady. 17 February 1694.

(PUPPET leaves. Space becomes more constrained. SOR JUANA remains 'broken' in the space.)

Scene Ten

(Shadows of ARCHBISHOP and BISHOP appear.
As the Puppeteer speaks SOR JUANA'S head becomes gradually disembodied and begins to rise, until she is finally above the room amongst the stars, moons and suns.)

SOR JUANA'S PUPPETEER
Despite this being considered a wondrous act by the Church, it seems to me the act of a terrified woman. Are we really to believe that the self-assured and witty woman of 1691 and 1692 turned into a passive penitent by 1694?

In giving up her music, her beloved books and denouncing her writing...her learning, she attempted to appease the wrath of Archbishop Aguiar y Seijas. An act of cowardice or courage?

She succeeded.
She lived for one more year under the complete domination of The Bishop, Nunez de Miranda, and The Archbishop, Aguiar y Seijas.

Her cell was left bare except for three small books of devotions and a number of hair shirts and scourges.

An act of cowardice or courage?
Whilst tending her fellow nuns during a severe epidemic she contracted the unknown disease.
At four o'clock on the morning of 17 April 1695 she died. Aged forty-six years and five months.

SOR JUANA
What concern have you, world, in persecuting me?
Why do I offend you, when all I desire
Is to give splendour to my mind
And not my mind to splendid things?

I do not care for possessions or wealth,
Being more content
To endow my mind with treasures
Rather than treasures with my mind.

And I esteem not appearance, which age
Removes in civil stealth.
You see, I am not impressed by wealth.

I believe in the truth that
The vanities of life are the better to expend
Than a life expended in vanities.

(Lights fade to Blackout.)

(The end.)

About the Author

Christine Roberts works as a Senior Lecturer in Theatre & Performance at the University of Plymouth, England. She is also a founder member of the theatre company Lusty Juventus. She has been writing professionally since 1996 and has had four of her plays performed nationally. In addition to this, she has also written for international journals and conferences on themes relating to theatre and politics. *Ceremonial Kisses* was the first play performed by Lusty Juventus and was selected by *The Times* as one of the highlights of the 1997 Edinburgh Fringe Festival; the company later performed this play in London, Bristol and Exeter. *Shading the Crime* was the second of her plays for Lusty Juventus and was later selected to open The Courtyard Theatre, Hereford in a production by Ellie Parker (1998). Other plays include *The Maternal Cloister* which was commissioned by Theatre Carnivalesque and was first performed as a rehearsed reading by Lusty Juventus in Brazil. Her first play, *Mangled*, was published by Minerva Press in 1997.

Lusty Juventus

Lusty Juventus physical theatre was founded in 1996 by Roberta Mock, Christine Roberts and Ruth Way. The company works collaboratively, drawing on the individual skills and talents of company members as performers, devisers, writers, choreographers, composers and designers. The company focus is on the production of politically committed new writing, choreography and composition. Besides the plays in this volume, Lusty Juventus produced the European premiere of Karen Malpede's *Us* in 1999. The company is currently working on its fifth project, entitled *M(other)*. The text is by Christine Roberts incorporating Algernon Swinburne's 'The Triumph of Time.'

Alisa, Alice
A play by Dragica Potocnjak,
Translated by Lesley Anne Wade

This play deals symbolically with the attitude of the European Union towards refugees, and specifically with issues of prejudice between two small nations with different religions, in the immediate context of a power relationship between a Slovenian and a Bosnian woman. This translation will contribute to an understanding of the relationship between the personal and the political, and provide insights into sources of prejudice, which inhabit our own lives.

Paper, 82pp
1-84150-104-2
£14.95

The Composition of Herman Melville
A play about writing and dramatic composition
By Rick Mitchell

The play, which contains bibliographical information relating to Herman Melville, is an explanation of the ways in which writers compose and are composed. Parallels between past and present (in racism, domestic abuse, and the plight of the visionary American artist) are clearly implied; but the play also utilizes new technologies, like video, in order to represent the kind of dialectical history and representation promoted by Benjamin.
The utilization of various performance strategies within the play generates the exposure of the complex textuality of a writer who has haunted the landscape of America from the mid-nineteenth century to the present.

Paper, 96 pp
1-84150-067-4
£14.95

Brecht in L.A.
An award-winning play by Rick Mitchell

Brecht in LA, winner of the 2002 SWTA National New Play Contest (US), is already a critically acclaimed play. Centering on Brecht while adapting and critiquing Brechtian dramatic form, the play provides a unique opportunity for the instructor who is teaching Brechtian theatre since - with just one text (which includes an essay on Brechtian performance, endnotes and appendices) - the instructor can cover epic theatre, the "Brecht debate," Brecht's biography, and contradictions between Brecht's theatrical practices and his everyday life.

Paper, 114pp
1-84150-105-0
£14.95

Intellect, in association with *Studies in Theatre & Performance*, publishes new writing for the theatre (or work that is new to U.K. audiences).
The publications in this series:
- promote tolerance, cultural exchange and dialogue through theatre;
- represent work that is aesthetically and/or stylistically innovative;
- may not be considered appropriate for production by 'mainstream' venues (in that they are experimental, risky, non-commercial, thematically or politically challenging, etc.);
- include contextualizing essays or author's notes to support the performance texts.
Please submit scripts, playtexts and/or performance writings that fit the above criteria to Roberta Mock, series editor, for consideration (r.mock@plymouth.ac.uk).

intellectbooks

Publishers of original thinking. PO Box 862 Bristol, BS99 1DE, UK www.intellectbooks.com